To Have and to Hold

DAVID ATKINSON

LIBRARIAN OF LATIMER HOUSE, OXFORD

To Have and to Hold

The Marriage Covenant and the
Discipline of Divorce

COLLINS
St James's Place, London
1979

William Collins Sons & Co. Ltd
London · Glasgow · Sydney · Auckland
Toronto · Johannesburg

First published in 1979

© David Atkinson 1979

ISBN 0 00 215528 1

Set in 11pt Monotype Imprint
Made and printed in Great Britain by
William Collins Sons & Co. Ltd

Author's Note

Latimer House, Oxford, is a centre for study and research. It is committed to the ideal of creatively applying biblical and Reformation theology to the ongoing life of the Church of England and the Anglican Communion.

This book is one of a series of occasional studies on theological subjects which bear on issues of importance for Anglicans today. It was first commissioned by the Latimer House Council to be a contribution to the current debate in the Church of England on the remarriage of divorced persons in church. In fact, the book's concerns are much wider than this one issue, and it is hoped that the discussion offered on the covenant nature of marriage and the ethical and pastoral questions raised by divorce and remarriage will be of much wider interest and usefulness. Some of the material was offered as a paper to the annual conference of the Church of England Reformed Fellowship in 1977.

I am very grateful for the help and constructive criticism I have received from members of the Latimer House Theological Work Group, and from the Warden, Revd Roger Beckwith, in particular.

December 1978   David Atkinson

Contents

CHAPTER I

Conflicting Trends in the Discipline of Divorce

The pain of a marriage breakdown is increasingly widespread and often unbearable and the Christian pastor needs wisdom and compassion in sharing in and ministering to a complex and difficult situation. For Anglican clergy the problem is complicated by different voices urging different pastoral responses to those who find themselves part of the tragedy of marital failure.

Other Churches have had a somewhat less rigorous approach to marriage breakdown than that indicated by the present Convocation rulings of the Church of England. The Church of Rome, for example, while maintaining very strict rules about divorce has a wide range of annulment procedures which acts as a safety valve for many situations of marriage breakdown. The Eastern Orthodox Churches recognize divorce for a variety of reasons, and second and even sometimes third marriages are solemnized in church. The Church of Scotland and most Free Churches have always allowed divorce and remarriage of certain persons, their pastoral procedures deriving, it is affirmed, from biblical principle.

The Church of England at present, however, makes no exceptions to a total ban on all remarriage in church after divorce, when a former partner is still living. This present practice defined in four Resolutions in 1938 and promulgated as an Act of Convocation in 1957,[1] is that 'according to God's

will, declared by our Lord, marriage is in its true principle a
personal union . . . indissoluble save by death; . . . as a consequence, remarriage after divorce during the lifetime of a
former partner always involves a departure from the principles
of true marriage . . .' and that in order to maintain the principle
of lifelong obligation,

> which is inherent in every legally contracted marriage and is
> expressed in the plainest terms in the Marriage Service, the
> Church should not allow the use of that Service in the case of
> anyone who has a partner still living.

Under certain conditions, however, 'recognizing that the
Church's pastoral care for all people includes those who during
the lifetime of a former partner contract a second union',
divorced and remarried persons may be admitted to Holy
Communion.

To many clergy this ruling is a wise one which witnesses on
the one hand to God's standard for marriage (by refusing
second marriage in church), and on the other hand to God's
grace (by making possible the welcome to Holy Communion).
To others this ruling seems an illogical compromise, adding
further pain and conscientious difficulty to the pastor with an
already painful task: for without doubt there are some persons
who having been through the trauma of a broken marriage now
realize all the more clearly what marriage commitment means
and who now – perhaps for the first time – want to call on God's
grace for a new start, but find that the Church is apparently
unable to share with them at the crucial moment. It is further
to be noted that a not insignificant number of those seeking to
marry a divorced person have not themselves been married
before, and they, too, are denied the Church's blessing. For
these reasons, there are some clergy who, contrary to Convocation ruling, avail themselves of the freedom granted in the
civil law, and do officiate at the marriage of some divorced
persons.

These differences of pastoral response are, however, just the present manifestation of the fact that it has never been possible to speak of *the* Church of England position on the question of divorce and right of remarriage. Behind today's pastoral questions lies a whole history of debate. The three central areas of difference are

(a) Alternative views about the nature of marriage. All are agreed that God's will for marriage is that marriage 'is in its nature a union permanent and lifelong, for better for worse, till death them do part, of one man with one woman, to the exclusion of all others on either side . . .'[2] The debate concerns whether a valid marriage once entered into on these terms can ever be broken in God's sight. Is marriage 'indissoluble' in fact?

(b) Alternative views about divorce. All are agreed that divorce is a grievous departure from God's will for marriage. But if a marriage cannot in fact be dissolved in God's eyes, whatever the courts of the land may declare, how is the Church to view divorcees? If, however, marriage can in some circumstances be dissolved, what – before God – counts as marriage breakdown?

(c) Alternative views about the function of the Church. All are agreed that the Church shall witness to God's truth both of his will for the permanence of marriage, and of the Gospel of grace and forgiveness. The difficulties come in trying to maintain the proper balance between its prophetic and pastoral responsibilities in its liturgical and disciplinary practice, against the background of differing views of ministry and sacraments.

These three areas of difference have been complicated in the last century particularly, by three other factors. The first of these is the changes in civil divorce legislation which have made State-recognized divorce increasingly more easy to obtain, and have seemed to some to force a division between civil law and Christian teaching. The second is the considerable social upheaval of recent decades, coupled with progress in psychological and sociological science, which have sometimes tended not only to make marriage more vulnerable, but have in many minds changed the whole understanding of what marriage means. The third is the development in biblical and theological scholarship which has to some degree altered the way questions about divorce have been asked and answered within the Christian Church.

We examine these briefly in turn, and then outline the main streams of Anglican pastoral thinking of recent decades.

(a) *Changes in civil law*

Before 1857 there was no legal provision in Church or State law for divorce, except by special Act of Parliament, the cost of which was prohibitively high for most people. According to A. R. Winnett[3] only 317 such special Acts were passed between 1670 (when the House of Lords passed a Bill to enable Lord Roos to remarry after divorce) and 1857. Half of these occurred after 1800. A Royal Commission of 1850 recommended that, among other things, divorce *a vinculo* should be available to a husband in the case of his wife's adultery, and that causes relating to marriage (apart from the issue of marriage licences) be transferred from ecclesiastical jurisdiction to special civil tribunals. The Commissioners believed themselves to be acting in accordance with the Matthean teaching in which Jesus seems to permit divorce 'for the cause of *porneia*', and as 'restoring the state of affairs in the latter half of the sixteenth century when, in their opinion, marriage was treated by the Church as dissoluble'.[4]

After extended Parliamentary debate, betraying a wide divergence of opinion among the bishops in the House of Lords, the recommendations of the Royal Commission became the Divorce Act of 1857. The Act was not without its critics within the Church, and certainly from that time the law of the land had departed from the old law of the Church expressed in the Canons of 1603 which only recognized separation *a mensa et thoro*, and forbade remarriage during the lifetime of a former spouse. A significant clause was introduced at one stage in the passage of the 1857 Bill through the House of Commons, providing that 'no clergyman in holy orders of the United

Church of England and Ireland shall be compelled to solemnize the marriage of any person whose former marriage may have been dissolved on the ground of his or her adultery'.[5] The implication of that provision, of course, is that many clergy would in fact do so.

This law of 1857, being based explicitly on the Matrimonial Offence of the wife's adultery, remained unaltered until 1937 when A. P. Herbert introduced a Matrimonial Causes Bill into Parliament. The Bill followed the majority view of an earlier Royal Commission of 1909, and extended the 'matrimonial offences' for which divorces could be granted to include desertion, cruelty, and incurable insanity. It also extended the grounds of nullity. Again, the following provision in the Bill is significant:

> No clergyman of the Church of England or of the Church in Wales shall be compelled to solemnize the marriage of any person whose former marriage has been dissolved on any ground and whose former husband or wife is still living or to permit the marriage of any such person to be solemnized in the Church or Chapel of which he is Minister.[6]

This protected the rights of individual clergy to act in conscience in this matter. If Convocation formulated a law that the clergy must remarry the divorced, this would be directly contrary to the Bill. (It is arguable that it is also contrary to the Bill for Convocation to legislate that they must not.) The Bill became law later that year, receiving support from some bishops and criticism from others.

The abuses to which the law based only on the 'matrimonial offence' was put are well known. Under growing pressure for reform of the civil law, the then Archbishop of Canterbury (Ramsey) appointed a group in 1964 to make recommendations on which the State's law of divorce could be made to work more equitably. The group, who carefully distinguished their task of making a Christian proposal for secular law from the Church's own discipline for its own members,[7] produced the Report *Putting Asunder* in 1966.[8] The Report proposed that 'the doctrine of the breakdown of marriage should be comprehensively substituted for the doctrine of the matrimonial offence as the basis of all divorce'.[9] This proposal became a significant part of the basis for the new civil Divorce Reform Act of 1969 (consolidated into the Matrimonial Causes Act 1973). The Act substituted the principle of irretrievable breakdown for that of matrimonial offence, but required the courts to be satisfied, as evidence of such breakdown, of at least one of the following facts: adultery which the petitioner finds intolerable; unreasonable behaviour by the respondent; two years' desertion; two years' separation with the consent to divorce of the respondent; five years' separation whether or not the respondent consents to divorce. This change in the law was made with the intention of providing a more equitable divorce law for a society in which marriage breakdown was becoming increasingly more common. The Church Assembly of 1967, in a long debate on Divorce Law Reform, welcomed the *Putting Asunder* Report 'and believes that the fact that a marriage appears finally to have broken down should be the sole grounds of civil divorce'.[10] Not all churchmen endorsed that welcome, however, nor the new legislation when it came in 1969. In effect the new law makes possible divorce by mutual consent (although arguably no more so than did the previous law, and without its injustices), and indeed allows divorce against the will of one of the partners if separation has been continuous for five years. This has been interpreted by some as making it impossible in English law now to contract a 'Christian marriage' (by which is meant an unbreakable union).[11] This interpretation is inaccurate, however, for the 1969 legislation is concerned with divorce, and does not affect the legal understanding of marriage in English law as expressed in an earlier judgement: 'the voluntary union for life of one man and one woman to the exclusion of all others'.[12] But there are confusions within the new law, and severely unsatisfactory features in its court procedures (to which we shall refer again in Chapter 5), which do give cause for serious doubt whether in actual practice the

1969 law is furthering the promotion of social justice as the signatories to *Putting Asunder* had intended.

One unmistakable result of the 1969 legislation is the astronomical rise in numbers of divorce petitions being granted.[13] While some of this may be accounted for by the 'regularizing' of many relationships which had for long been a hollow shell, but for which divorce was not possible under the old law, this is not the whole story. The primary social question here is to what extent availability *creates* demand. It is not surprising that many within the Church have assumed that not only is the rise in divorce figures one more indication of the fact that society is losing its moorings, but also therefore that the primary Christian duty is at all costs to maintain the standard of the absolute indissolubility of marriage, and that this is to be expressed by a total hostility towards all divorce and towards the remarriage of any divorced persons in church. The problem is far from being that simple, however. Apart from the ambiguity in its use of the term 'indissoluble' (we shall argue that it can properly be used of the moral obligation for permanence in marriage; its common use to mean an unbreakable *vinculum* cannot, I believe, be sustained), the Church has other callings to fulfil than simply the prophetic role of proclaiming standards. Furthermore, as Helen Oppenheimer notes, the present refusal of the Church of England to remarry divorcees while welcoming them to Communion can often belie in practice what it is intended to proclaim:

> In principle we are refusing to bless what Christ deplored; in practice we are refusing to make up our minds whether to affirm in Christ's name that certain actions must always be deplorable.[14]

The Church is called to be, among other things, the agent of the mission of Christ in contemporary society: that mission includes proclaiming and creating the possibility for the living out of God's will for marriage. It also includes being the minister of reconciliation, forgiveness and the new start in situations of personal failure. It is the difficulty of finding the balance in these tasks which adds to the confusion of pastoral opinion within the Church of England at the present time.

(b) Upheavals within society

While to some extent it is true that changes within the law create changes within society, the momentum is at least as strong in the other direction. The rapid social changes affecting the role of marriage within the family and within society, and indeed the understanding of what marriage means have themselves contributed to the calls for reform in the laws regulating divorce. Today's problems are not only centred in the *avant-garde* fringe who see the breakdown of the whole concept of marriage and family as inevitable and as progress. They are centred in the changing character of modern marriage itself. It goes without saying (almost) that the cultural environment of our day is very different from that of biblical times. This is seen not only in the changed and changing status of women in our society, the different financial considerations (the dowry system, the bride price, etc.) and the different legal structures of society. As Thielicke puts it, it is seen also in the fact that before the period of Romanticism, the marriage contract was the responsibility of the family and people often married or were married with the hope that love would arise within the marriage bond; in modern times, however, the individual eros has grown to be the standard criterion for determining whether two persons are 'created for each other', and people marry on the basis of love already felt.[15] The pastoral problem for the Church of England includes that of how to relate its understanding of the biblical teaching concerning God's will for marriage to the upheavals within contemporary society which are constantly posing new questions, and reframing old questions in new terms. In his authoritative book *Marital Breakdown*,[16] the Christian psychiatrist Dr Dominian comments on some of these recent social and psychological factors which, working on each other, have tended to make the marriage relationship increasingly more vulnerable.

As well as the social impact of two world wars, for example, this century has witnessed changes in family patterns. Until the industrial revolution, says Dr Dominian, marriage and the family formed a 'cohesive unit centred on the home' which was the site of both production and consumption.[17] Now, the separation between the husband's, and now many wives', work and their home, the increase in State involvement in what were previously family functions (like education), the breakdown of patriarchy and the increasing emancipation of women, have all contributed together to put a different value on the marriage relationship. The priorities are now much less ordered in terms of marital rights and duties, than in terms of companionship and complementarity. The quality of the personal relationship, and the satisfaction of personal needs, are now – particularly in these post-Freud times – much more significant within marriage.

Alongside these social changes, Dr Dominian notes the fact that people live longer, marry younger and, with increasingly effective contraceptive facilities available, have smaller families. 'Thus the actual amount of time devoted to child-bearing has been drastically reduced, freeing wives for other activities and experiences, which means a return to work and a much greater emphasis on the quality of the relationship between the spouses.'[18] Furthermore, other qualitative changes in the character of life have been made possible: Dr Dominian puts it like this: 'As the issues which have concerned humanity from time immemorial, namely the conquest of disease, pestilence, material poverty and the ravages of nature, are gradually coming under control (there is still a long way to go and we must ensure that we do not create new ones like pollution or total depletion of primary resources), the next layer of being which involves the wide-scale implementation of freedom, justice, personal dignity, emotional growth and healing are assuming increasing importance.'[19]

These factors, coupled with the insights of modern psychology (and the preoccupation of much modern thinking with the meaning of sexuality), have forced changes in the questions about marriage from the functional ones which occupied Christian thinking in previous centuries ('What is marriage for?'), to the relationship-centred questions ('What does marriage mean?, What is the role of sexuality within a person's life and relationships?').[20]

The effects of such changes can cut two ways. On the one hand, marriage, says Dr Dominian, 'is the structure which manifests the widest range of opportunity for . . . personal fulfilment'.[21] And in another place, speaking of the wounds of personality with which many come to married life:

> In the intimate experience of marriage there is . . . opportunity to heal these wounds in the exchange of love, where one partner can give to the other as far as possible what is missing . . .

> Modern marriage has precisely the intimacy and closeness which allows each spouse to experience afresh through each other their past and thus be given a new opportunity to receive and learn the missing component from their previous experience . . .[22]

On the other hand, when fulfilment becomes its own goal, this can lay on marriage burdens too great to bear. Concentration on the 'next layer of being, the psychological, emotional and sexual' not only opens 'new vistas' in the relationship between partners in marriage, but simultaneously makes 'greater demands'.[23] Commenting on the sorts of psychological distress which have their primary cause in human selfishness, and the prevalent attitude that 'I have a right to have everything as I want it', Professor Stanley Strong says this:

> Unfortunately our materialistic culture encourages all of us to be sharply aware of the slightest deprivation and to expect, even demand, its fulfilment. We believe that we are not adequately living unless our lives are stuffed full of gratification. A source of great unhappiness is the secular teaching of our society that everyone must lead an active sexual life indulging in sex wherever, whenever, and with whomever we wish. When we are not 'fulfilled' as we have been led to expect, we have a 'right' to become upset . . . Others do not always deliver, and when they do, the

demander is seldom happy for he has only received what he had a 'right' to expect, and since he demanded it, it does not have a satisfying quality of genuineness.[24]

The concentration on the quality of the marriage relationship has also made increasingly significant the psychological and sexual problems which make relationships difficult. Although marriage can be, and ideally should be (as Dr Dominian says) the sphere within which partners suffering pain can be helped towards healing, it can also (as Dr Strong's paper argues) be the context in which such pains become exposed, and can be inflamed by 'selfishness' and so work for destruction rather than growth.

Such trends within marriages will mean different things in the different social and economic contexts in which marriages are made. In R. Holman's criticism of the 'distance' between the Lichfield Report (*Marriage and the Church's Task*) and the 'working class population' (published in *Shaft*, Winter 1979), the author stresses the influence of continuing socially depriving conditions on the stability of marriage. These factors also need to be built into the Church's (and nation's) thinking about marital breakdown. He isolates four in particular:

First, the pressure to marry young is greatest on 'members of the lower social classes'. (Single people are not usually given council houses; there is the desire to escape cramped homes; the wish for privacy with a loved one; the expectation of the need to make room for younger children. There is also, notes Holman, a significant correlation between early marriage and the experience of social deprivation.)

Second, financial poverty can put unbearable strain on a marriage. ('Anxiety about rent, worry about whether the electricity will be cut off, having to say "no" to children when they want to go on the same school excursions as their friends, can lead to situations where husbands and wives blame each other.')

Thirdly, the effect of unemployment does more than create financial hardship. The husband's sense of feeling de-valued, and some wives blaming their husbands for their unemployment; increase in boredom and loneliness; all these can be linked to breakdown in personal and marital relationships.

Fourthly, Holman underlines the fact that severe illness or handicap can contribute to marital problems, and significantly 'members of social class V are particularly vulnerable to severe illnesses', and are at the same time least likely to possess financial and housing resources which may off-set some of the pressures. 'Clearly, their marriages are thus subject to stresses unknown to many more affluent couples.'

Such factors as these, and there are others too, are part of the complex of upheavals in today's society, and undoubtedly contribute to the vulnerability of marriage, and to the increase in the numbers who resort to the divorce courts. How is the Christian Church to react to such complex changes and personal needs, and maintain its calling to witness to God's will for the permanence of marriage? Many Christians now realize that it is not sufficient simply to denounce divorce. Alongside that realization they hear the sociologist R. Fletcher even suggesting that increased resort to divorce need not indicate any decrease in the stability of family life. 'On the contrary, it could indicate (a) a bringing out into the open a recognition, in and through the law, of a social actuality (whatever its unsatisfactory aspects) which had long existed but which had hitherto been prevented from formal resolution, and (b) a *raising* of the standards expected of marriage, and an active will to end the unsatisfactory and move towards the more satisfactory.'[25] This corresponds with Richard Jones's comment on Jewish communities which have for long had liberal divorce laws, and yet this has not meant that Jewish family life has been noticeably unstable; rather the facility to terminate bad marriages and promote good ones could well ensure strength to family living.[26]

On the other hand, many argue that availability *does* create demand, and the more people resort to divorce, the more divorce becomes acceptable as a solution to marital unhappiness. Commenting on American society in *The Social Context of Marriage*, J. Richard Udry ascribes the high divorce rate to the current conception of marriage as only an arrangement of mutual gratification, a conception which is itself fostered by increasing use and availability of divorce. 'The kind of marriage Americans believe in simply has high divorce rates.'[27]

The response of the Christian Church cannot be content with the proclamation of standards; it must come to grips with the personal and pastoral difficulties in making those standards realizable within the changing features of our culture and society. It must come to grips also with the social situations which magnify those difficulties.

The task for the Church is likely to become yet more urgent if the thinking of some psychologists and sociologists, who regard the whole conception of marriage and family as antagonistic to the well-being of humanity, becomes more widespread (not to mention the future effects that trivialized 'sex without any relationship' in contemporary pornography may have on the attitudes to marriage of the next generation).[28] The psychologist R. D. Laing, for example, and his disciples, developed what has been described as a 'scathing criticism of the "family" as the most bland, vicious and repressive social structure yet devised'.[29] They are primarily warning against the psychological pressures which can exist within the emotional tightness of the small modern family.

The sociologist J. Bernard, in *The Future of Marriage*, believes that, though the institution of marriage can have a future, it will of necessity be very different from the idea of an exclusive life partnership of one man with one woman. That will simply be 'one option among many' for the way people choose to spend their time and 'tailor their relationships to their circumstances and preferences'.[30]

How does the Church find the balance between seeing the divorced person as sinner and seeing the divorced person as victim in a society like this?

(c) *Trends in biblical scholarship*

The third complicating factor contributing to differences of pastoral approach within the Church of England concerns the Bible. Until the development of biblical critical scholarship, the controversies on the questions of divorce and remarriage centred almost entirely on the interpretation of the *porneia* clauses in Matthew's Gospel (5:32; 19:9), and of the Pauline Privilege (1 Cor. 7:15). The Continental Reformation tradition understood the former as an exception from the lips of Jesus to his otherwise total prohibition of divorce and remarriage (as Mk. 10:11 and Lk. 16:18 were understood), and what Winnett calls[31] the 'non-indissolubilist tradition' within the Church of England argued from this that divorce was legitimate on grounds of the wife's adultery (many extending this to the husband's adultery also, on the basis of the apparent equalizing of the woman's status in Mk. 10:12). The pre-Reformation Western tradition had argued, on the contrary, that Jesus was not referring to divorce *a vinculo* at all, but to separation *a mensa et thoro*, and that Matthew was simply recording the permission for that sort of separation on grounds of adultery. Such a view is upheld in the Anglican Canon Law of 1603. The Pauline Privilege had also been understood by the Reformed tradition within the Church of England as permission for divorce and possibly remarriage in a mixed marriage when a Christian was deserted by an unbelieving partner.

Some critical scholarship of the last eighty years has cast doubt on the word used for 'separation' in 1 Cor. 7; it might only refer to temporary living apart and not divorce *a vinculo*. More seriously, the *porneia* clauses in Matthew were relegated in much critical thinking to a secondary strand in the Gospel tradition, and were not believed to come from the lips of Jesus at all.

Thus Bishop Gore (1911) said that 'the critical conclusion that the exceptive clause in the first Gospel is an interpolation, which really alters the sense of our Lord's original utterance about marriage, and that His real teaching is that given in St Mark's and St Luke's Gospels, represents an impressive consensus of scholars from Germany, France, America and our own country – a consensus of scholars moreover, who, as being mostly Protestants in conviction, were predisposed in favour of the laxer view of the marriage bond'.[32] This view of the *porneia* clause has become common orthodoxy until fairly recently when some commentaries seem less hasty to reject its authenticity as words of Christ.[33] In the first decades of this century, the indissolubilist tradition within the Church of England, strengthened by the fact that most scholars generally held that the exceptive clause was a contradictory Matthean addition to the teaching of our Lord, became dominant, and a rigorist rejection of all remarriage after divorce prevailed.

There was another divergence, however, within theological scholarship which also contributed to lack of consensus within the Church of England on the biblical material. With the authenticity of the Matthean exceptive clause disputed, the question at issue became rather the nature and purpose of the teaching of Christ: was he giving prescriptive legislation, or was he setting forth an ideal and a principle, the application of which needed to be worked out by his followers in their contemporary situations? Indissolubilists like Bishop Gore held to the view that Jesus was giving a specific law. 'Against those who say that He was only stating an ideal and not promulgating a law, I should urge that His saying was never understood except as a commandment addressed to the Christian conscience such as must form the basis of a specific law.'[34] Dr Hastings Rashdall, on the other hand, while also rejecting the authenticity of the Matthean exception, represented a more liberal view:

> The difficulty which we experience in determining what our Lord actually taught on this matter, impressively illustrates the absolute impossibility of basing detailed rules for the guidance of modern life upon isolated sayings of Christ. That the ideal is permanent monogamous marriage is undoubtedly the principle which Jesus taught . . .

By what detailed enactments the ideal may best be promoted, which is the less of two evils when that ideal has been violated and made impossible, is a question which must be settled by the moral consciousness, the experience, the practical judgement of the present . . .

Our Lord's prohibition of divorce, even if the exception is removed, is not more peremptory, as far as the letter goes, than His prohibition of oaths, of self-defence, or of going to law.[35]

These trends within scholarship, contributing to the lack of a consensus within the Church of England on the question of divorce, are to be assessed alongside the differences of emphasis within the Church of England on the authority of the Bible itself. There have always been exponents of the 'Reformed' position of the Church of England, exemplified by Cranmer himself. Even in the case of learned and godly-minded men, he argues 'we are to believe them no further than they can show their doctrine and exhortation to be agreeable with the true Word of God written. For that is the very touchstone which must, yea, and also will, try all doctrine or learning whatsoever it be, whether it be good or evil, true or false.'[36] His letter to Osiander on the question of the second marriage of Philip of Hess[37] shows himself to be in line with Peter Martyr's desire to submit to biblical authority on the question of divorce. Martyr writes:

As I for my part with all my heart embrace those causes which be expressed in the Scriptures, so can I hardly endure that divorcement should stretch beyond these bounds.[38]

For comparison we cite one speaker in the Church Assembly debate on Divorce Law Reform in 1967, for whom biblical authority is not the only issue:

We are not a Bible Church; We are based, most of us would agree, on the Bible as our chief and prime authority, but in this matter we must consider both tradition and reason . . .[39]

Likewise the Root Report, *Marriage, Divorce and the Church*

(1971), found the biblical material inconclusive; 'the solution to our problem must be found by an evaluation of factors other than purely biblical considerations'.[40]

These divergences of view about the meaning and the authority of the biblical material, and its application to contemporary needs, have contributed, alongside the rapid cultural changes which this century has witnessed, and the associated changes in civil divorce law, to the persistent lack of a theological consensus within the Church of England on the question of divorce and remarriage.

Anglican Pastoral Discipline

It is not surprising in such a context as we have outlined, that there have been different proposals urged on the Church of England for its pastoral discipline for its own members on the question of divorce and remarriage. There seem to have been four main options:

(i) The 'rigorist' view

Probably the most influential view this century, certainly in the earlier years, was that expressed by T. A. Lacey in 1912 in his book *Marriage in Church and State*.[41] He argued that marriage is 'in the order of nature' indissoluble except by death.

> If marriage were a mere contractual relation, an artificial partnership, it would be terminable not only by a failure to achieve its object, but even more equitably by mutual consent; because it is constituted in the order of nature, and not only at the will of the parties, it is indissoluble except by an event equally in the order of nature, and this can be found only in death.[42]

Lacey, and Mortimer (in his revised edition of Lacey's book) argue that this is the constant teaching of Christianity, and that it is not only Christian marriages, 'raised by grace to the status of a sacrament', but all marriages that are indissoluble by natural law.[43] The only divorce that can be countenanced therefore is separation *a mensa et thoro*, and all question of remarriage is invalid, because the legal decree which regulates separations should not be thought to dissolve the bond of valid marriage.

K. E. Kirk[44] likewise speaks of the 'indissolubility of marriage by natural law', though he is less inflexible about the difficulties of pastoral practice than is Lacey. His primary objection to all remarriage is that it 'bars the door against all possibility of reconciliation'.[45] The Lambeth Conference of 1930 recommended that 'the marriage of one whose former partner is still living shall not be celebrated according to the rites of the Church'[46], a view which was strengthened in the Resolutions of Convocation of 1938, which became the Act of Convocation of 1957 defining present Anglican discipline: 'the Church should not allow the use of that Service (the Marriage Service) in the case of anyone who has a former partner still living'.[47]

This view was also expressed in the Convocation debate on the proposed revised Canon 36 (in September 1950). Canon Lindsay Dewar, for example, changed the wording of one amendment from 'indissoluble' to 'permanent'. His intention was to make clear that what was meant was 'absolute indissolubility' ('*indissolubilis*', he said, 'constantly occurred in the writings of the Canonists') rather than the meaning 'ought not to be dissolved', which was gaining currency. He drew the House's attention to Appendix IV of the Report of the Joint Committees of the Convocations of Canterbury and York on the Church and Marriage, 1935, which included:

> It is the almost unanimous opinion of scholars consulted that the 'exceptional clause' in Matthew 5:32 and 19:9, is in neither place part of the original teaching of our Lord.

It was beyond reasonable doubt, said Canon Dewar, that our Lord's teaching was that marriage was permanent in nature, not permanent as an ideal.[48]

This 'rigorist' line has been recently defended in *For Better, For Worse*,[49] and *The Theology and Meaning of Marriage*,[50] and

has been upheld in the Synod debates in 1972 and 1978
following the publication of the two Reports: *Marriage, Divorce
and the Church* (1971) (Root) and *Marriage and the Church's
Task* (1978) (Lichfield). The difficulty of this rigorist position
arguing against the *possibility* of divorce from 'natural law', is
that marriages are in fact dissolved. Even scholars of the Church
of Rome which affirms the absolute indissolubility of marriage,
recognize that arguments from 'natural law' need to be qualified
by the fact that dispensations for dissolution are granted.[51] The
rigorist view is also based on the conviction (which we believe
to be wrong) that Jesus taught that marriage was absolutely
indissoluble. It is a clear call for Christian standards to be
maintained in a moving society; it is another question whether
its standards are more rigorous than those of Christ.

(ii) The 'legislative' view

A second view seeks to do justice to the belief that the New
Testament gives a law for marriage in absolute terms, but does
allow exceptions in its application. One exception (usually
understood as adultery) in Matthew's Gospel, and the other
(desertion by an unbelieving partner) allowed in 1 Corinthians
by Paul, are the basis upon which Christian discipline must
be based. R. H. Charles[52] allowed divorce with right of
remarriage on these grounds, Bishop Chase[53] did on grounds of
adultery only. At the Oxford Conference on Marriage and
Divorce in 1956, the legitimacy of divorce on grounds of
adultery and desertion was defended by J. Stafford Wright.[54]
In his reply to the Root Report, J. R. W. Stott also argued for
the propriety of divorce after adultery, with right of remarriage,
and that a believer may aquiesce in the desertion of his or her
unbelieving partner. He then adds: 'We should have the courage
to resist the prevailing tide of permissiveness and to set ourselves against divorce and remarriage on any other ground than
the two mentioned . . .

'We may on occasions feel at liberty to advise the legitimacy
of a separation without a divorce, and even a divorce without a

remarriage taking 1 Cor. 7:11 as our justification. But we have
no liberty to go beyond the permissions of our Lord.'[55]

The difficulty with this view is that in pastoral practice it *can*
lead to the sort of casuistry which can become negatively
legalistic. It concentrates on physical adultery but neglects
other 'unfaithfulness', and can mean that the Church's blessing
for second marriage is reserved only for those who are fortunate
(!) enough to have had their former partner commit adultery
against them. It raises the question as to what breaks the
marriage bond.

(iii) The 'double standard' view

In 1944 A. T. MacMillan published a book[56] in which he argued
for the recognition of two sorts of marriage: those solemnized in
church with the declaration of the intention of permanence,
which should be regarded as indissoluble, and those solemnized
before a registrar which would not be regarded by the Church
as indissoluble. Such a procedure would certainly make the
pastoral problems a great deal clearer, but it would, as Bishop
Kirk said, 'suggest something of which neither Church nor
State has ever heard: either the full vows have been exchanged
in due form and then there is a marriage, or they have not and
then there is none'.[57] It is one of the fundamental affirmations of
Christian belief about marriage that it is, in the words of the
older theologies, a 'creation ordinance', and that, as *Marriage
and the Church's Task* puts it rightly 'it is more appropriate to
speak of "a Christian doctrine of marriage" than of "a doctrine of
Christian marriage'."[58] Whatever happens subsequently, it is the
consistent view of both Church and State that valid marriage is
intended to be permanent. Any sort of 'double standard' view
which seeks to distinguish a law for marriage for Church
members from the law for marriage for those outside the
Church, does not do justice to the fact that marriage is not a
Christian idea, but is part of the way God has structured his
creation.

(iv) The 'more liberal' view

Hastings Rashdall[59] was one of the clearest exponents of the view that whereas 'indissolubility' means that marriage *ought not* to be dissolved, some nevertheless are broken, and that although divorce is sin, it may sometimes be the lesser of two evils. This sort of view was upheld by the minority group of the 1935 Report of the Joint Committees of Convocation,[60] including scholars like Bishop Barnes. It was supported by Bishop Chavasse,[61] and by among others,[62] Dr Sherwin Bailey in *The Mystery of Love and Marriage* (1952),[63] and more recently Helen Oppenheimer in *The Marriage Bond* (1976),[64] who have both argued that remarriage after divorce should be permitted in certain circumstances in which the marriage relationship has irreparably broken down.

The Root Report of 1971[65] and the majority view in the Lichfield Report of 1978[66] were both critical of the 1957 Convocation rulings as being too rigorist, and both argued for the remarriage of divorced persons in church under certain circumstances. The Root Report recommended that if there exists in the country a moral consensus about the propriety of allowing that some marriages could 'die' while the partners were still alive, that consensus should be read as part of the theological data in considering whether and in what circumstances remarriage in church could in some circumstances be allowed. The view of the Commission was that such provision should be made, and proposals for a penitential procedure be held before any second marriage service were given.

The Lichfield Report agreed with the main conclusions of the Root Commission, though more adequately argued, but instead of a change in the service proposed a preliminary pastoral procedure requiring episcopal permission for each application for remarriage. Neither Commission sought to distinguish between persons whose marriages had broken down for different reasons.

Other critics of the Act of Convocation ruling have included

Canon A. P. Shepherd,[67] F. Dulley,[68] H. Oppenheimer[69] and
G. R. Dunstan.[70] There was a minority dissenting group in the
Lichfield Commission however, who argued in favour of the
present ruling. As one of their members, J. R. Lucas, had
already said in print:[71] 'What will come over' (if the Church
decides to take a more liberal line) 'is that the Church has
abandoned its traditional loyalty to our Lord's teaching and
accommodated its doctrine to the needs of modern man.' As he
argues later:

> The tension between the Church's pastoral and prophetic roles
> cannot be fully resolved ... It is one thing for the Church to be a
> Servant Church ... it is another to be an accessory to sin ...[72]

It is that tension to which this present paper is addressed.
How is the Church of England to fulfil its prophetic and pastoral
roles at a time of rapid social upheaval and associated changes
in civil law – a task made more difficult by prevailing uncertainty
about the biblical revelation? These factors pose again the
questions: (i) What makes a marriage? What is the response of a
biblically informed morality to the changing understanding of
the meaning of marriage in our society? and (ii) What breaks a
marriage? What response should the Church, seeking to uphold
a biblical morality, make in situations of marital breakdown?
These questions we shall look at in turn, seeking to expound
the biblical description of marriage as covenant, and attempting
to evaluate the moral force of the biblical teaching on divorce.
It is our conclusion that the present Anglican discipline does not
adequately express biblical principle nor does it provide a
realistic pastoral procedure.

But first, it will be appropriate to set the present Anglican
discussion within the context of earlier centuries and the wider
Church, and offer a brief historical sketch of the main trends in
Christian thinking.

SUMMARY OF CHAPTER I

1 The present Anglican Convocation ruling, banning church remarriage after divorce when a former partner is still living, is valued by some as a wise pastoral compromise; others believe it conceals part of the Gospel of forgiveness.

2 The question concerning the Church's attitude to divorce has been complicated by (a) changes in civil law, making for easier divorce; (b) social upheavals reframing old questions in new terms, and requiring new responses; (c) trends within biblical scholarship which have required a closer look at the New Testament divorce material.

3 There have been four main options in Anglican pastoral discipline in recent decades: (i) the 'rigorist' view, that marriage is absolutely indissoluble; (ii) the 'legislative view', that divorce is permitted for certain causes; (iii) the 'double standard' view, that Christian marriage is indissoluble, but State marriage may not be; (iv) the 'more liberal' view, which sees divorce in some circumstances as the lesser evil.

4 Is the present Anglican discipline adequate biblically and pastorally?

REFERENCES TO CHAPTER I

1 *The Chronicle of Convocation*, No. 2 (1957) p. 205f, esp. p. 211.
2 Canon B 30: 'Of Holy Matrimony', *The Canons of the Church of England* (1969).
3 A. R. Winnett, *Divorce and Remarriage in Anglicanism* (Macmillan, 1958), p. 129.
4 Winnett, *op. cit.*, p. 139.
5 *Ibid.*, p. 144.
6 *Ibid.*, p. 231.
7 *Putting Asunder, A Divorce Law for Contemporary Society* (SPCK, 1966), para 6.
8 *Op. cit.*
9 *Op. cit.*, para 26.
10 Church Assembly *Report of Proceedings* (Feb. 1967), p. 253.
11 Cf. for example 'The Undermining of Marriage' by E. W. Trueman Dicken in Cheslyn Jones (ed.), *For Better, For Worse* (CLA, 1977)[2].

12 The Judgement of Lord Penzance in *Hyde v. Hyde* (1886).
Cf. also Nachimson v. Nachimson (1930), quoted in *Marriage and the Church's Task* (CIO, 1978), p. 23. The signatories to this Report give their considered judgement that the Divorce Reform Act of 1969 has not in any material way altered the law's understanding of what is required of a valid marriage. (*Op. cit.*, p. 29).

13 The Report *Marriage and the Church's Task* quotes the following statistics (thousands, England and Wales):
Numbers of marriages: 1966: 384.5; 1972: 426.2; 1975: 380.6.
Divorce decrees made
absolute: 1966: 39.1; 1972: 119.0; 1975: 120.5.
Richard Jones in *How Goes Christian Marriage?* (Epworth, 1978), quotes: Divorce rates per 100 married population:
1911: 0.07; 1966: 3.20; 1972: 9.50; 1976: 9.50.
The rate of remarriage amongst divorced people also appears to be rising rapidly.

14 H. Oppenheimer, *The Marriage Bond* (Faith Press, 1976), p. 84.

15 H. Thielicke, *The Ethics of Sex* (James Clarke, 1964), p. 102.

16 J. Dominian, *Marital Breakdown* (Penguin, 1968)

17 *Op. cit.*, p. 9.

18 J. Dominian in *Marriage, Divorce and the Church* (SPCK, 1971) appendix, p. 143.

19 J. Dominian, 'The Changing Nature of Marriage and Marital Breakdown', *The Clergy Review* (Dec. 1973), p. 930.

20 Cf. R. Jones, *How Goes Christian Marriage?* (Epworth, 1978), p. 78.

21 J. Dominian, *The Clergy Review* (Dec. 1973), p. 930.

22 J. Dominian, *Cycles of Affirmation* (Darton, Longman and Todd, 1975), p. 62.

23 J. Dominian, 'Marital Breakdown' in *Marriage, Divorce and the Church* (SPCK, 1972), p. 143.

24 S. R. Strong, 'Christian Counselling', *Counselling and Values* (1975).

25 R. Fletcher, *The Family and Marriage in Britain* (Penguin, 1973), p. 153.

26 Richard Jones, *How Goes Christian Marriage?* (Epworth, 1978), p. 75.

27 J. Richard Udry, *The Social Context of Marriage* (Lippincott, 1966), p. 526, quoted in E. L. Hebden Taylor *The Reformational Understanding of Family and Marriage* (Craig Press, 1970).

28 Although Richard Jones, *op. cit.*, quotes statistics to support the

view that even the shift in attitudes towards a more sexually experienced younger generation is not necessarily linked at all with any undermining of marriage or the sense of responsibility and satisfaction which most persons find within it (p. 33).

29 R. Jones, *op. cit.*, p. 42, referring to R. D. Laing, *The Divided Self* (Penguin, 1961) and *The Politics of the Family* (1976), and especially cf. David Cooper, *The Death of the Family* (Pelican, 1972).

30 J. Bernard, *The Future of Marriage* (Penguin, 1972), p. 281f.

31 A. R. Winnett, *op. cit.*

32 C. Gore, *The Question of Divorce* (John Murray, 1911), p. 23. Cf. also *Hastings Dictionary of Christ and the Gospels* (1906); *The New Commentary on Holy Scripture* (1928) on Matt. 19:9: 'almost all scholars are now agreed that the exceptive clauses here and in 5:32 were never spoken by (our Lord)'.

33 K. Stendahl, *Matthew* in *Peake's Commentary on the Bible* (1962), on Matt. 5:32; D. Hill, *Matthew* (Oliphants, 1972).

34 C. Gore, *op. cit.*, p. 46.

35 H. Rashdall, *Conscience and Christ* (Duckworth, 1916), p. 106.

36 T. Cranmer, *A Confutation of Unwritten Verities* in *Works* Vol. 2 (Parker), p. 14, quoted in P. E. Hughes, *The Theology of the English Reformers* (Hodder, 1965), p. 36.

37 Dated 1540; printed in *The Work of Thomas Cranmer* by G. E. Duffield (ed.) (Sutton Courtenay, 1964).

38 P. Martyr, *The Commonplaces* (1583), p. 458.

39 Church Assembly *Report of Proceedings* (Spring 1967), p. 243.

40 *Marriage, Divorce and the Church* (SPCK, 1971), p. 95.

41 T. A. Lacey, *Marriage in Church and State* (SPCK, 1912), fully revised and supplemented by R. C. Mortimer (1947).

42 *Op. cit.*, p. 15.

43 *Ibid.*, p. 16.

44 K. E. Kirk, *Marriage and Divorce* (Hodder and Stoughton, 1933).

45 *Op. cit.* (1948 edition), p. 135. Cf. also A. H. Box and C. Gore, *Divorce in the New Testament: a reply to Dr Charles* (SPCK, 1921).

46 Quoted in Winnett, *op. cit.*, p. 214.

47 See ref. 1.

48 *The Chronicle of Convocation* (Sept. 1950), p. 414.

49 Cheslyn Jones (ed.), *For Better, For Worse* (CLA, 1977)[2].

50 *The Theology and Meaning of Marriage* (CLA for The Church Union, 1978).

51 Cf. D. O'Callaghan, 'Theology and Divorce' in *Irish Theological Quarterly*, *37* (1970), p. 212.

52 R. H. Charles, *The Teaching of the New Testament on Divorce* (William and Norgate, 1921).
Charles found difficulty with St Paul's apparent forbidding of remarriage (and came to regard 1 Cor. 7:11 as an interpolation). From the Gospels, he argued that Christ allowed right of divorce on ground of adultery as well as remarriage for the guiltless person, but forbade divorce and remarriage on any lesser grounds. Christ's statements on divorce, he argued, condemned only those who put away their wives on inadequate grounds. Charles understood 1 Cor. 7:15 to concede right of remarriage to a deserted believer.

53 F. H. Chase, *What did Christ teach about Divorce?* (1921).

54 J. S. Wright, *Church Gazette* (Nov.-Dec. 1956), p. 13f.
J. Stafford Wright argues that the Matthean exception must be taken as authentic, and be presupposed by Mark and Luke, and takes 1 Cor. 7:15 'is not bound' to mean a believer 'is free to remarry', after desertion by an unbelieving partner.

55 J. R. W. Stott, 'The Biblical Teaching on Divorce', *The Churchman*, *85/3* (1971), p. 165.

56 A. T. MacMillan, *What is Christian Marriage?* (Macmillan, 1944).

57 Kirk, *op. cit.*, p. 30.

58 *Marriage and the Church's Task* (CIO, 1978), p. 31.

59 Rashdall, *op. cit.*

60 Joint Committees of Convocations, *The Church and Marriage* (1935).

61 C. M. Chavasse, *Five Questions Before the Church* (Canterbury, 1947).

62 E.g. J. H. Cruse and B. S. W. Green, *Marriage Divorce and Repentance in the Church of England* (Hodder, 1949).

63 D. Sherwin Bailey, *The Mystery of Love and Marriage* (SCM, 1952).
Dr Bailey argues that the basis of the marriage bond is the 'one flesh' union, and therefore where the personal relationship has irreparably broken down the marriage is an 'empty shell'. Release can only come by repentance. 'Instead therefore of allowing remarriage after divorce to the "innocent" party as many have wished . . . it seems that it ought rather to be permitted to the repentant and to them only.' p. 96.

64 H. Oppenheimer, *The Marriage Bond* (Faith Press, 1976).

65 *Marriage, Divorce and the Church* (SPCK, 1971).

66 *Marriage and the Church's Task* (CIO, 1978).

67 A. P. Shepherd, *Marriage Was Made for Man* (Methuen, 1958).

68 F. Dulley, *How Christian is Divorce and Remarriage?* (Grove, 1974).

69 *Op. cit.*, and papers in *Theology* esp. May 1975.

70 G. R. Dunstan, *Theology*, May 1975 editorial, quoting also *The Artifice of Ethics* (SCM, 1974).

71 J. Lucas, 'Frustration and Forgiveness' in *Theology* (May 1971).

72 *Op. cit.*

CHAPTER 2

Historical Sketch

The divergences of view on the legitimacy of divorce and right of remarriage within the Church of England can be seen on the wider canvas of the whole history of the Christian Church. It is not our purpose to attempt a complete history (the reader is referred to the fuller treatments of e.g. Watkins, Joyce, Winnett, Schillebeeckx),[1] but rather to sketch some of the more important phases of Christian thinking and focus the questions for contemporary discussion which the thinking of earlier generations poses.

(a) The Early Centuries

There are few references to divorce in the writings from the first three centuries, and such as there are have been variously interpreted.

G. H. Joyce, examining the writings of early Christian writers and canons of the early councils concludes that in the Roman Empire until Justinian 'the attitude of the Church was unwavering . . . alike in East and West she maintained with absolute consistency that divorce is altogether impossible. It is often assumed', continues Joyce, referring primarily to Basil (c. 360) and Epiphanius (c. 403), 'that some of the Fathers adopted a somewhat laxer attitude, and that there are indications of a divergence of view on the subject, at least in the Eastern Church.' This contention Joyce believes to be 'devoid of any solid foundation'.[2] This is also the opinion of Anglican Bishop Gore. 'Is it the case', he asks, 'that the Church has consistently or generally held that Christian marriage is an indissoluble bond which even adultery does not abolish?' He answers: 'That was certainly the mind of the primitive Church – the Church of the first three centuries.'[3]

Other historians are not so certain. The Churches of the East look to certain Fathers of the early centuries in support of their belief that divorce and remarriage are lawful under certain conditions. It is particularly noteworthy that even in the Roman Catholic Church, which has usually looked to early tradition in support of its absolute indissolubilist position, some recent writers have claimed that tradition is 'not sufficiently clear' to decide the question of the indissolubility of the marriage bond. In *Divorce and Remarriage*, for example, V. Pospishil argues that although a majority of Fathers and ancient ecclesiastical authorities generally denied remarriage to all wives – even 'innocent' – none the less remarriage was permitted to husbands of adulterous wives.

> There are no witnesses of the early Church – as long as we do not lose sight of the necessary distinction among related legal concepts – which would support the present Catholic doctrine on the indissolubility of sacramental marriage.[4]

And again:

> While the first centuries yield only a few references favourable to divorce neither do they furnish testimony to its absolute exclusion. It is therefore to be expected that a condemnation of divorce as a moral evil would be sometimes displayed, although there was no doctrinal principle formed as to its legal implications (Hermas, Clement of Alexandria, Ambrose of Milan).

> Whenever we encounter a prohibition of remarriage after divorce, it *first* is directed to wives, while there is no mention of husbands and their legal situation; or *second*, divorce is declared permissible solely because of adultery, or *third* divorce is disapproved for specific causes other than adultery. (Justin Martyr, Origen, Cyprian, Hilary of Poitiers, Gregory of Nazianzus, Chromatius of

Aquileia, John Chrysostom, Jerome, Theodoret of Cyprus . . .)[5]

After Constantine, divorce-remarriage is more frequently mentioned, and while on the one hand the Fathers sought strongly to oppose certain features of contemporary civil practice (e.g. divorce by mutual consent), on the other hand (so Pospishil interprets the evidence) 'the right of a husband to divorce an adulterous wife was always upheld, and he was considered justified in marrying another woman. (Origen, Lactantius, Basil, Ambrosiaster, Asterius, Epiphanius, Victor of Antioch, Aritus of Vienna . . .)'

This Catholic writer thus believes that the passages from the Fathers which have usually been interpreted (with Joyce and Gore) as evidence for a unanimous rejection of the possibility of divorce with right of remarriage, have been misunderstood. What these passages really offer is a strong argument from silence: it is the absence of any explicit prohibition of divorce and remarriage that is striking.

> The absence of a concerted and systematic fight by the Eastern Church against imperial legislation permitting divorce ought to be interpreted as reflecting the mind of the Church – different from that of the Catholic Church today – that divorce was not prohibited by the law of Jesus.[6]

Pospishil's work has been severely criticized by the French theologian H. Crouzel.[7] He criticizes Pospishil's presuppositions, and on the contrary contends that it cannot be proved that the Fathers allowed remarriage; indeed, he argues, the texts of the age show clearly that one cannot argue from any presumption in favour of new marriage. No ancient source, with the exception of Ambrosiaster, permits the remarriage of husbands of adulterous wives. Pospishil's book is not only badly argued, but historically inaccurate. Likewise, continues Crouzel, the common assertion that the present discipline in the Eastern Church concerning divorce and remarriage was substantially that of the Greek Fathers of the fourth and fifth centuries is 'simply false'.

On the subject of divorce, the first Christian centuries do not merit the scepticism with which they are sometimes regarded, because in East and West they show a real unity in the exegesis of the Scriptural texts and in the discipline which results.[8]

Pospishil replied to these criticisms[9] quoting a fairly substantial group of Catholic scholars who affirm that 'there are numerous voices from the early Church attesting the practice of permitting the remarriage of some divorced persons'. The ancient texts are capable of different interpretations, and Pospishil accuses Crouzel of starting from the premise that 'indissolubility must somewhere be hidden in the saying of the writer'. He quotes Montserrat Torrens as saying 'Catholic theologians since Trent refuse to accept such a gross contradiction on the part of the Fathers of the Church and they accordingly deny they admitted such an exception. This they do by forcing an "orthodox" meaning on the old texts favouring remarriage so that they cease to contradict the current practice of the Church of Rome.'

Pospishil's own view is described as 'possibly one of the more careful summaries' in Cheslyn Jones (ed.), *For Better, For Worse*.[10]

While such arguments belong within careful historical study, it appears that the evidence from the early Fathers may be capable of differences of interpretation, and it would be difficult to use such evidence as an unambiguous indication that the teaching of Jesus is rightly to be understood as prohibiting divorce in all circumstances.

It is instructive at this point to notice the way the teaching of the Fathers was used at the time of the Reformation: it was not primarily an assessment of the correct exegesis of Scripture, but was rather used in support of dogmatic and moral arguments. Thus Peter Martyr in his *Commonplaces* (to which we refer later) lists five commonly argued 'causes why the Fathers would that new marriage should not be lawful after divorce was made for fornication's sake'. Of these, three are arguments of moral expediency: that a husband might be tempted to

invent adultery to get a divorce; that after one marriage failure
it would be unwise to 'try the same luck again'; that it might
tempt an unhappily married man to 'feign to be a heretic' so
that he might get his marriage annulled. The two other biblical
arguments (from Romans 7 and 1 Cor. 7, and from the saying
'That which God hath coupled together let no man separate')
Martyr believes do not rule out divorce with right of remarriage
in all circumstances.

We shall look at the importance of Peter Martyr later. For
the present, we turn back to Augustine who is usually regarded
as giving the fullest exposition of the absolute indissolubility of
the marriage bond, and here we find the evidence posing for us
some important questions. Whether we regard Augustine's
view of the sacramental and therefore indissoluble nature of
marriage as 'something of an innovation' which even in the
West remained largely disregarded for a while, though it was
later to be translated and developed into what is now Catholic
orthodoxy[11] or whether, with Joyce,[12] we regard Augustine's
position as identical with (though perhaps the fullest exposition
of) the consistent witness of the Fathers, there is no question
that his treatment of the nature of marriage as a 'sacrament' had
a vast influence on the whole Church.

We clearly cannot devote space to Augustine's (largely
unfortunate) exposition of sexuality, and can only refer briefly
to the three 'goods' of marriage as he expounded them. The
first 'good' of marriage is offspring; the second is 'fidelity' or the
guarantee of chastity; the third is the pledge or sacramental
bond.[13]

By 'fidelity', Augustine means both the negative 'restraint
and remedy for sin' which preserves mankind in its fallen
condition, to restrain concupiscence within the bonds of
marriage, and also – as he saw it – the positive remedying of the
'sinfulness of concupiscence' within marriage. Despite his
largely negative attitude to sexuality, therefore, he none the less
saw marriage as exercising a positive function within God's
redemptive purpose.

The third 'good' of marriage is the sacramental bond. And here it is important to note that while the first two 'goods' of marriage (namely progeny and the 'faith of chastity') are 'goods' of 'natural' marriages, the third good 'pertains unto the people of God'.[14]

Augustine says nothing about the permanent and indissoluble qualities of marriage under the heading of the first two 'goods'. He finds grounds for 'indissolubility' in the nature of the sacramental bond, the good that belongs especially (does he mean only?) to marriage between Christian partners. Indissolubility consists in the 'sanctity of the sacrament'.[15] 'For this is preserved in the case of Christ and the Church, so that as a living one with a living one, there is no divorce, no separation for ever.'[16]

The sacramental bond is therefore the imprint upon natural marriage of Christ's indissoluble bonding of himself to his people.

Exegetically in Augustine the reference to marriage as a sacrament is based above all on Eph. 5:22 where the Vulgate translates *musterion* as *sacramentum*. We shall in the next chapter need to consider further whether or not it is right or helpful to speak of marriage in sacramental terms. We are concerned here with making the point that it is to Augustine primarily that the Western Church of later centuries and the Catholic tradition of today owe the designation of marriage as a sacrament, and the corollary drawn in the Catholic tradition that the marriage bond is therefore absolutely indissoluble. Having said that, however, we need to draw out the two important questions which Augustine's exposition poses.

First, as we have said, Augustine did not argue for the indissolubility of marriage from the first two 'goods' (progeny and marital fidelity) – or what later theologians might call Natural Law. He does not describe marriage in its natural state, while recognizing its place in God's intention for society, in the language of indissolubility. That is a term appropriate for marriages which show the third 'good' (*sacramentum*), namely, as he would see it, marriages between Christian believers. This raises the question for us, therefore, whether or not it is true that (to use Joyce's words[17]), 'Christian marriage stands on a different plane from marriage among the unbaptized . . . Christian marriage possesses a special title to indissolubility'.

Whatever our answer to the technical question as to whether or not marriage is a sacrament, we need also to face the question whether it is the response of marriage partners to the love of Christ, and the ordering of their lives under his redemptive grace that is the strengthening factor which *alone* suggests and sustains the ideal of indissolubility, and by which the ideal becomes a reality.

The second question of importance is the sense in which Augustine uses the term '*sacramentum*'. Following the Vulgate rendering of Eph. 5:22, Augustine calls marriage a *sacramentum* by which he means both an indissoluble bond of 'sacral obligation', and also a sacred sign of the union between Christ and his Church. *Sacramentum* is a technical Latin term for the Roman soldier's oath – that which places him under an obligation[18] and it is in that sense of moral obligation and sacred sign that Augustine uses the term (and not in the later medieval sense of the sacrament of marriage as an ontological bond). As Schillebeeckx comments:

> Augustine's view of marriage . . . was that the partners in marriage had a lifelong obligation to remain faithful to each other because of the obligations undertaken in the marriage contract, but these obligations were all the more binding because the marriage was a *sacramentum* or sign of the mystery of Christ in the church, and so because in the case of infidelity something sacral was violated.[19]

In other words, indissolubility for Augustine was a matter of 'life commitment', an 'oath of fidelity', and it was therefore *not permissible* to dissolve a marriage, since marriage involved a personal commitment to live married life in such a way that the bond of marriage was not broken.[20]

This places marriage under the *moral obligation* of permanence, a bond which *should not* be dissolved. This is rather

different, however, from the later scholastic concept of the
'*sacramentum*' as an 'ontological participation in the covenant
between Christ and his Church', and therefore an objective
bond which once validly made *could not* be broken.[21]

To draw together some of the threads of discussion so far,
therefore, we have concluded that the evidence from the earliest
centuries is open to difference of interpretation, and that even
in Augustine, one of the clearest early exponents of the indissolubility of the marriage bond, the question arises especially
(only?) for Christians, and is primarily one of moral impermissibility rather than one of ontological impossibility.

(*b*) *The Eastern Church*

What is less open to difference of interpretation is the evidence
that after the beginning of the sixth century there was a divergence between the Greek and Latin Churches on the possibility
and therefore permissibility of divorce with right of remarriage.

The Greek Episcopate did not insist on the absolute indissolubility of the marriage bond; the Eastern Church was
ready to accept the civil law of divorce embodied in the Codes of
the Roman Emperor Justinian (AD 536); and the rulings of the
Penitentials of Theodore of Tarsus (c. 690) allow divorce and
remarriage on the lines of the civil legislation in force in the
Empire.

Some commentators regard this as a continuation of the
position of some of the Fathers (Origen, Basil in particular) for
whom the remarriage of divorced persons can be said to be
justifiable in some cases as the lesser of two evils, although
contrary to the Scriptural ideal for marriage.[22]

Others (e.g. Joyce[23]) who interpret Origen, Basil and others
as in fact upholding the divine law of the indissolubility of
marriage, regard the practice of the Eastern Church from the
sixth century as an increasingly lax and inexcusable departure
from this law.

The Eastern Church today seeks, with what it believes to be
precedent from long tradition, consonant with the teaching of

Scripture, to hold with one hand to the strict view of marriage as a sacrament (administered by bishop or priest) which in its ideal is an organic union so close that it is not dissolved even by death,[24] and to hold with the other hand to the authority of the Church, in exercising loving care towards believers who transgress canonical ordinances, to grant permission for remarriage after divorce.

Divorce and remarriage is now permitted as a concession to men's hardness of heart, for a variety of causes. In the Greek Orthodox Church in the USA, for example, divorce may be granted and remarriage permitted, after adultery or other gross immorality, attempt on life, abortion without husband's consent, continuing impotence, desertion for two years, apostasy, incurable insanity, leprosy.[25]

(c) The Roman Tradition

By contrast with the practice of the Eastern Church, the Latin Church held increasingly firmly to the law of the absolute indissolubility of the marriage bond, believing this to be the law of Christ, and believing it so to have been interpreted throughout early tradition, particularly by Augustine.

As we have noted, however, at the time of the Fathers, marriage was a bond of permanent moral obligation. By the time of the medieval schoolmen, indissolubility had come to mean in addition an ontological *vinculum* which *could not* be broken – at least in respect of consummated marriages of baptized believers. One can point to some relaxations of the absoluteness of this law in the intervening centuries,[26] but the reforms of Hildebrand at Cluny ended these concessions and (to quote Winnett),

> The *Decretum* of Gratian, compiled shortly before the middle of the twelfth century, laid down that a consummated marriage admitted of no dissolution. The marriage bond could not be severed by adultery, and still less by other causes. Though separation for adultery was permitted, remarriage was forbidden. From the time of Gratian to the Reformation, the doctrine of

indissolubility was unquestioned in the Western Church, at least in respect of the consummated marriage of Christians.[27]

Marriages contracted by unbelievers were in certain cases capable of dissolution. Innocent III had at the end of the twelfth century embodied the 'Pauline Privilege'[28] into the canonical legislation of the Church.

The Roman Church has subsequently always affirmed the authority of the Church to dissolve marriage unions which were either not consummated, or involved an unbaptized person, under certain conditions.

It was in the twelfth century also, that the question as to when a marriage comes into being was given its classic answer. Alexander III affirmed that at least for Christians, consent rendered a marriage valid, and consummation rendered it indissoluble, a symbol of the union between Christ and the Church. This is fundamentally the position in the Roman Catholic Church today.[29]

This marriage law of the medieval Church was very strictly upheld. Alongside it, however, grew up a complex system of 'impediments' which allowed for the growth of the practices of dispensation and annulment. These all too easily became means of escape from burdensome marriage, and it is largely against these practices that the Reformers were to protest in their rejection of the doctrine of absolute indissolubility.

None the less, it is the same law of absolute indissolubility that underlies the declarations of the Council of Trent (1545-63); it was given expression by Pope Pius XI in the Encyclical *Casti Connubii* (1930), and was more recently upheld by the Second Vatican Council (1962-5).

All three of these Statements need a brief comment.

Trent

At the Council of Trent, the Roman Church made a more formal and explicit declaration than she had ever yet delivered.[30] As against the Reformers, who denied the sacramental nature of the marriage bond, and sought Scriptural support for the lawfulness of divorce with right of remarriage in certain circumstances (as we note later), the Council of Trent affirmed that

> The first parent of the human race, under the influence of the divine spirit, pronounced the bond of matrimony perpetual and indissoluble, when he said *This is now bone of my bones, and flesh of my flesh. Wherefore a man shall leave father and mother and cleave to his wife, and they shall be two in one flesh.* But that by this bond two only are united and joined together, our Lord taught more plainly, when rehearsing those last words as having been uttered by God, He said, *therefore they are not two but one flesh* and straightway confirmed the firmness of that tie, proclaimed so long before by Adam, by these words: *What therefore God hath joined together, let no man put asunder.* But the grace which might perfect that natural love, and confirm that indissoluble union, and sanctify the married, Christ Himself, the institutor and perfector of the venerable sacraments, merited for us by His passion . . .[31]

In other words, natural marriage is here perfected and confirmed in its indissoluble state by the grace which Christ merited for us, and even natural marriage is perpetual and indissoluble by virtue of the 'one flesh' union which is created in marriage. We shall need to ask further of the meaning of 'one flesh', and query whether this does in fact imply absolute indissolubility, or whether rather it refers to God's creation ideal and intention for marriage.

The Council of Trent then propounded twelve Canons on Matrimony, anathematizing among other views, those that the bond of matrimony might be dissolved by heresy, 'irksome cohabitation', desertion, and that the Church had erred by teaching that marriage cannot be dissolved on account of adultery (Canons V and VII); the view that the Church could not 'establish impediments dissolving marriage' (Canon IV), and the view that 'solemn profession of religion' (entry into religious order) did not dissolve an unconsummated union (Canon VI).

This seems clear enough, but it is worth noting that behind the conciliar statements, there was no absolute unanimity among the bishops. The Catholic writer Pospishil even believes that the negative way in which the Canons are cast may be sufficiently ambiguous to justify doubt whether the pronouncements of Trent can be used conclusively to assert that the Roman tradition is unambiguously committed to the absolute indissolubility of the marriage bond.[32]

Casti Connubii

The prevailing discipline of the Church of Rome today was summed up by Pius XI in 1930 in his encyclical on Christian marriage.

> (*Section 5*) Matrimony was . . . established by God; . . . God the Author of nature and Christ our Lord, the restorer of nature, provided marriage with its laws . . . consequently those laws can in no way be subject to human wills . . . This is the teaching of Sacred Scripture; it is the constant and universal Tradition of the Church; it is the solemnly defined doctrine of the Council of Trent, which uses the words of Holy Scripture to proclaim and establish that the perpetual indissolubility of the marriage bond, its unity and its stability, derive from God Himself.

> (*Section 31*) The complement and crown of all is the blessing of Christian marriage which, following St Augustine, we have called SACRAMENT. It denotes both the indissolubility of the matrimonial bond, and the consecration of this contract by Christ, who elevated it to the rank of a sign which is a cause of grace. The indissolubility of the marriage contract is emphatically declared by Christ Himself . . .

And then in a further section, noting again the distinction which in some circumstances is drawn between consummated marriages of Christians, and marriage unions which are either not consummated, or involve an unbeliever:

> (*Section 34*) If the stability of marriage appears in some rare cases to be subject to exception – as in certain natural marriages contracted between infidels, or between Christians, in the category of marriages ratified but not consummated – such exception does not depend upon the will of man or of any merely human power, but upon the divine law, of which the Church of

Christ is the sole guardian and interpreter. *But no such dissolving power can ever, or for any cause, be exercised upon a Christian marriage ratified and consummated.* In such a marriage the matrimonial contract has attained its final perfection, and therefore by God's will exhibits the highest degree of stability and indissolubility, which no human authority can put asunder.[33]

Vatican II

The Statement of the Second Vatican Council on this question follows the same theme. In *Gaudium et Spes* we read that 'the intimate partnership of married life and love . . . established by the Creator and qualified by his laws' is 'rooted in the conjugal covenant of irrevocable personal consent'.

> Hence by that human act whereby spouses mutually bestow and accept each other, a relationship arises which by divine will and in the eyes of society too, is a lasting one. For the good of the spouses and their offspring as well as society, the existence of this sacred bond no longer depends on human decision alone . . . This intimate union . . . imposes total fidelity on the spouses and argues for an unbreakable oneness between them.[34]

The same theme, but is the language somewhat less uncompromising than *Casti Connubii*? The stress here is more on the obligation of permanence, but the language of 'sacred bond' and 'unbreakable oneness' still seems to imply an ontological *vinculum*.

Further, in *Apostolicam Actuositatem*, it is urged as a 'supreme task' on Christian couples 'to manifest and prove by their own way of life the unbreakable and sacred character of the marriage bond'.[35]

While, therefore, the official position of the Roman Church seems to maintain both the moral obligation and the ontological *vinculum* of the indissolubility of marriage, there is sufficient ambiguity for discussion. Indeed, in recent years the history and doctrine of the Roman Church's divorce discipline (particularly the possibility of the dissolution of the marriage bond 'in favour of the faith' – i.e. for spiritual reasons) has come up for a good deal of debate.[36]

At the fourth session of Vatican II, the Archbishop Zoghbi suggested that the Church's practice of dissolution might be extended beyond the limits referred to in *Casti Connubii*. 'There is here an exegetical, canonical and pastoral problem which cannot be ignored. It is a matter for the Church to decide on the opportuneness of admitting a new cause for dispensation analogous to those which she has introduced in virtue of the Petrine Privilege.'[37]

This lead from Archbishop Zoghbi was taken up by Father Pospishil in the work already referred to. He believes that the Scriptures may well allow for divorce under certain conditions, such as adultery, as the Reformers argued. As we have noted, he finds the testimony of the early Fathers inconclusive, and the pronouncements of Trent ambiguous. He further believes that the official Catholic doctrine is not defined *de fide*,[38] and he argues that a distinction must be maintained between 'intrinsic' and 'extrinsic' indissolubility. While Scripture and the Fathers are unambiguously clear that partners to a marriage are not able themselves, and should not therefore legally be entitled themselves, to dissolve their marriage ('intrinsic indissolubility') this is a different matter from 'extrinsic' indissolubility, in which some authority outside the marriage can dissolve the marriage. It is Pospishil's argument that God has vested such authority in the Church 'by the power of the keys', and that the Church is therefore authorized to use that power to dissolve certain marriages under certain conditions. Further, in the face of what is now known from modern sociological and psychological, as well as theological debate, the Church ought from compassion and realism, to use that authority, and the rigorous discipline summed up by Pius XI ought to be relaxed.

The vast majority of modern Roman Catholics no doubt, would have difficulty with Pospishil's view, but he is by no means alone in seeking to find some way within the Church of Rome to make provision for the recognition of divorce, and the right of remarriage in certain circumstances.[39]

(d) The Continental Reformers

The Reformers in seeking to recall the Church to biblical principles, found themselves at variance with contemporary marriage doctrine and pastoral practice. Doctrinally, they rejected the elevation of marriage into a sacrament, with its corollary of absolute indissolubility, and argued on Scriptural grounds for the lawfulness of divorce *a vinculo* with right of remarriage in certain circumstances (the circumstances differed in the teaching of different men). Pastorally, they objected to the growth of the complex medieval procedures of dispensation and annulment by which burdensome marriages were becoming all too easily dissoluble in fact, by overcoming or evading the law of indissolubility. This brought the whole divine ideal of permanence into disrepute. Both doctrinally and pastorally, therefore, the Reformers agreed in abandoning the principle of absolute indissolubility which had been upheld in the Western Church during the Middle Ages. And they believed that in doing so, they were recalling the Church to the Scriptural teaching on marriage and divorce. This is not to say that they abandoned the divine ideal of permanence in marriage, nor indeed failed to insist on it as a moral obligation (as we have interpreted Augustine). Rather, they upheld that ideal and that obligation very strongly. They did, however, allow that while the marriage bond *should* not be dissolved, there were Scriptural grounds on which dissolution could be legitimate though not mandatory, and the right of remarriage upheld. (Only a very few regarded divorce as *mandatory* in these circumstances.)

We shall ourselves discuss the Scriptural material in detail later (Chapters 3, 4), and at this point simply illustrate the departure from Western tradition in the Continental Reformers, with examples from a few representatives.

Luther, in *The Babylonian Captivity*, gave three main objections to the elevation of marriage into a sacrament in the teaching of the Church of Rome; the theological argument that marriage contains no *particular* sign which requires marriage to be regarded as a sacrament (though, to be sure it is 'sign-like'), and nowhere does Scripture promise grace simply through the process of becoming married; the phenomenological argument by which Luther affirms that true marriage is not the monopoly of the baptized but is rather a worldly institution within the world created and preserved by God; and the exegetical argument that the Vulgate translation of *musterion* by *sacramentum* provides no basis for speaking of marriage as a sacrament in the theological sense.[40]

Once marriage was stripped of its sacramental character, its jurisdiction and discipline passed, so Luther taught, from the Church to the State. Luther also interpreted the words of Christ in Matt. 19 as permitting divorce for the cause of fornication, and after such a divorce, remarriage should be allowed. He further maintained, on the basis of 1 Cor. 7:15, the lawfulness of divorce for malicious desertion, and he interpreted this fairly widely to include the refusal of conjugal rights, and the refusal of reconciliation in domestic quarrels.[41]

Marriage, Luther believed, is *ipso facto* dissolved by the action of the guilty party in adultery, and the divorce court judge merely declares that fact. While the law of Christ (admitting divorce on the two grounds only of adultery and desertion) binds the consciences of believers, Luther allowed the State the right to legislate as is best for the whole community and this would allow recognition of even wider grounds for divorce (such as cruelty) to be legal.

Calvin's position was somewhat more strict. He, like Luther, allowed that adultery and desertion were grounds for divorce, though 'desertion' was more strictly interpreted as such. Remarriage was allowed to the innocent party after divorce in the case of adultery, on the grounds that the adulterer was held to be a dead person, and death dissolves the marriage bond. If the offender was allowed to go on living, it was the fault of the civil magistrate who was unwilling to enforce the law of God which prescribed death for adultery.

In commenting on the exceptive clause in Matthew 19, Calvin says:

> But the exception which Christ states appears to be superfluous. For, if the adultress deserve to be punished with death, what purpose does it serve to talk of divorces? But as it was the duty of the husband to prosecute his wife for adultery, in order to purge his house from infamy, whatever might be the result, the husband who convicts his wife of uncleanness, is here freed by Christ from the bond. It is even possible that, among a corrupt and degenerate people, this crime remained to a great extent unpunished; as, in our own day, the wicked forbearance of magistrates makes it necessary for husbands to put away unchaste wives, because adulterers are not punished. It must also be observed, that the right belongs equally and mutually to both sides, as there is a mutual and equal obligation to fidelity.[42]

Calvin and the Calvinistic Churches thus, like Luther, assigned jurisdiction over marriage to the State, but unlike Luther, Calvin held that the State was accountable to God to administer the law as revealed in Scripture as being obligatory on all.

According to Joyce, by 1561 Calvin had widened his opinion on the meaning of Paul's teaching in 1 Cor. 7, and granted divorce on the score of adultery, desertion, incorrigible vagabondage on the part of the husband, and strong presumption of adultery on the part of the wife.[43]

Of the Continental Reformers who came to England, Martin Bucer was perhaps most 'lax' in his teaching. His views are found in *De Regno Christi*, written for and dedicated to King Edward VI,[44] though even his friends regarded them as dangerous.[45]

Bucer's reply to those who forbade remarriage after divorce, was that Moses permitted it, and Christ came not to destroy the law but to fulfil it. To regard the marriage bond as existing apart from the actual sharing of bed and board and 'all other loving and helpful duties' is hypocritical. Bucer expounded the essential nature of the marriage bond in the words 'The twain shall be one flesh', and from this he argued that where such union was absent 'either by obstinate malevolence, or too deep inbred weakness of mind, or through incurable impotence of body', no marriage bond truly existed and divorce was permissible. Bucer therefore allowed divorce not only for adultery and desertion, but also for serious crime, impotence, leprosy and insanity.

If Bucer was held to be rather a lax extremist, the other major Continental figure to come to England, Peter Martyr, was, to judge from references to him in the writings of the English Reformers, held in the very highest esteem.[46] Martyr gave perhaps the fullest systematic exposition of the doctrine of marriage and the question of divorce of any of the Continental Reformers, and after his arrival in Oxford in 1547 and his close association with Archbishop Cranmer, he became one of the most important and influential teachers of doctrine in the English Reformation. Before discussion of the Church of England's attitude to divorce, therefore, it is important to give space to Peter Martyr. The English translation of his *Commonplaces* appeared in 1583, and it is in Part 2, Chapter 10 that he discusses Matrimony and then 'Divorcements'.

In the first place, Martyr is clear about the divine ideal of permanence in marriage:

> Although that copulation be separated by adultery, yet when the matrimony is contract, both man and wife ought to have this in their mind: that being once joined, they must abide and live together.[47]

And again, after discussion of concubinage, and polygamy:

> I verily when I ponder with myself these words 'In one flesh', I perceive great emphasis or force in them. For 'one flesh' is either by colligation as when all the members be knit one with another, or else by continuation. Both the ways make that all the parts of the body to serve one another . . . We see therefore that by the force of the words, both adultery and polygamy are taken away. But thou wilt object: Why then in a divorce, by reason of adultery, is it permitted to have another marriage? I answer: For that the

cause of the unity is taken away, and that is the fastening together
. . . But he which committeth adultery, cleaveth not unto his
wife, and so he is not one flesh with her . . .[48]

The principal point of matrimony is friendship, and friendship
doth chiefly consist in justice – and if justice halt, matrimony
must needs be lame . . . Wherefore, the husband cannot marry a
second wife without injury done unto the first.[49]

That same sense of moral obligation for permanence underlies the way Martyr handles the lawfulness of divorce for
adultery, and possibly desertion:

Unto the Hebrews and Ethniks it was but a light matter to put
away their wives, and it was lawful upon every occasion; but unto
Christians it ought not so to be. This hath Christ declared in the
5th and 19th of Matthew . . . (he) calleth us home unto the first
institution. For insomuch as now the Spirit is more plentiful,
and grace more abundant, men ought to use greater patience and
charity towards their wives, and not so to deal against them as they
should reject them for every cause. In like manner there is
required of the wives a greater obedience and modesty . . .

And touching the sentence that matrimony should not be
dissolved, Christ allowed it by a testimony out of the book of
Genesis: 'For this cause a man shall leave his father and mother,
and shall cleave unto his wife' Gen 2:24. Two near friendships
are laid together . . . and as the bond of amity between the child
and the parents endureth perpetually, so doth the conjunction
between the husband and the wife . . .

Yet he will have the cause of adultery excepted. And Paul (by
whom Christ speaketh) excepteth another thing, namely if one of
the married persons, in that he is an infidel, will not dwell with
the other being faithful, as it shall be declared in place, convenient.[50]

Then, against those who are 'bold to say' that the meaning of
the exception for adultery 'was to comprehend therein all other
wickedness', Martyr argues that Christ meant adultery only (in
Matthew 19:9 and 5:32), and

for my part, as I with all my heart embrace those causes which be
expressed in Scripture, so can I hardly endure that divorcement
should stretch beyond these bonds.[51]

Martyr is also very clear that 'nothing ought to be adventured' in the question of divorce, 'except the magistrate do ratify the same', and he urges therefore that the civil laws of the land be brought into conformity with the Word of God on this question. Those who take the law into their own hands incur severe punishment. Where, however, the laws of the land do not allow divorce, what is the Christian man to do?

> Certainly there are but two remedies which he must have recourse unto: that either, when he is driven to this strait he may now think that he is called unto this single life by God, whom by continual prayers he ought to move and solicit, that he will be present with him, whereby he may live chastely and purely; and when he perceiveth injury is done unto him by the laws, let him commend his cause unto God, for that he did not wilfully and of his own accord cast himself into this state . . . *But*, and if he shall altogether perceive that he is not able to live a chaste and continent life and that he cannot be persuaded in his mind to live single and without a wife; and thinketh it expedient for him to use the liberty which God hath appointed, lest he should do it against the will of his own magistrate, and against the common laws; let him depart and get himself into other countries where this may be lawful, there let him marry.[52]

We note that divorce for Martyr meant *a vinculo*, and not, as the Roman Church had interpreted the Matthean exception, simply 'from bed and board':

> This moreover ought to be certain, that Christ, when he excepted the cause of adultery, meant not a divorce wherewith the wife and husband should be separated only (as they say) from the bed and board, and that the bond of wedlock should still remain. The Lord spake unto the Hebrews, wherefore his words are to be understood of the usual divorce amongst that people. Also the Ethniks as well as the Romans and Grecians had only this sort of divorce known among them; that the one married person was so loosed from the other as new marriages might be lawful.[53]

Finally, on the question of remarriage, Martyr is clear that theologically speaking, divorce includes permission to remarry. It is instructive to give account of his disagreement with 'those causes why the Fathers would that new marriage should not be lawful' even after divorce 'made for fornication's sake': There were, as we noted earlier, five such causes:

First for that it might seem that the husband lusting after a new wife would invent a feigned crime of adultery against the first. Further, for that it might seem no wise man's part that when it happened ill with him before he would try the same luck again, and after a sort seek the same infelicity. Besides these, there are brought in the places as well to the Romans as to the Corinthians where the apostle seemeth to be of that mind: that a wife so long as her husband shall live is bound to his law. The latter writers also do cavil that matrimony is a sacrament and that therefore it cannot be made void. And Innocentius when he decreed that it is not lawful for the one party married to enter into new matrimony, if the other shall be fallen into heresy, addeth this reason: that there would be a door open into great inconvenience, for any man would soon feign himself to be a heretic that he might be delivered of his wife and obtain another. Further, they be wont to urge this saying: 'That which God hath coupled together, let no man separate.'

These reasons Erasmus doth plainly confute:

Touching the first: If a sever judgement be appointed by bishop or magistrates, false reports might easily be prevented neither will there be any leave given of divorce unless that fornication shall plainly and evidently be proved.

Of the other reason it is said: That which is objected is very ridiculous, seeing we oftentimes see that those which have failed once without good success and have abbidden shipwracke, do return again to shipping.

And the party which is innocent, while he endureth pickings and burnings and cannot easily keep himself chaste: what marvel is it if he cast in his mind to marry again?

Touching the place to the Romans it may easily be answered: The apostle did not there dispute whether divorcements might by any means be admitted, but it sufficed him . . . to show that it was now lawful to marry again in Christ after that death was come, which is the certain and undoubted cause of dissolving matrimony . . . Very wisely therefore did Paul in that place put only the cause of dissolving matrimony which of necessity he was to grant, although no other cause had happened in the meanwhile.

But whether matrimony be a sacrament or no is not hard to be answered. If thou understand the name of a sacrament generally and at large for every such thing as signifyeth some holy thing, we will not deny but that matrimony may be a sacrament, seeing it resembleth unto us the conjunction of Christ with his Church . . . But after this manner thou art forced to appoint not only seven but an infinite number of sacraments . . . But if thou wilt draw the name of a sacrament to those things which not only betoken spiritual things but also are used to be done by certain words and of which there is a commandment extant that they should be done, in this sense thou canst not appoint matrimony . . .

A slender reason also is that Innocentius brought, for by the like and same reason might any man feign himself to be a servant when otherwise he were free to the intent he might undo the matrimony contracted and procure himself another wife. And if that the error of that State were so great a matter to them that it dissolved matrimony, why should not that be of more force which Christ himself and the apostles did except.

Neither doth that greatly trouble us which they uttered in the last place, namely that it is not man's part to separate them whom God hath put together. For when such causes as there be do happen, it is God which divideth and not men, for so much as he by his word hath given this power.[54]

We can summarize the position of the Continental Reformers as best exemplified by Peter Martyr, therefore, in four main points. First, they upheld and proclaimed the divine ideal and moral obligation of the permanence of marriage. Second, they were united in holding the lawfulness of divorce *a vinculo* for adultery and malicious desertion (and a few extended the grounds to include cruelty (Luther), and even disease (Bucer)). Third, they believed that the jurisdiction of marriage discipline and divorce provisions should be in the hands of the State. Fourth, they believed that when a divorce was lawfully granted, this was coupled with right of remarriage.

(e) The Church of England

Two books were published in the 1950s which sought to summarize the thinking of the Church of England on the doctrine of marriage and the question of divorce, from the Reformation onwards. One of these, R. Haw, *The State of Matrimony*,[55] concentrates on the official formularies, the Prayer Book, the Canons, the practice of Church Courts, the Resolutions of Convocation. On this basis he argues that the Church of England has consistently throughout her history adhered to the concept of marriage which 'it received from pre-Reformation Western Christendom'[56] namely that marriage is a sacramental status, an indissoluble union,[57] which 'cannot be dissolved save by death'.[58] That the official formularies can, and some must, be interpreted in this way is not disputed, though we shall argue that in some cases Haw's interpretation – particularly of Cranmer's thought – is questionable. What is hidden by Haw's approach, however, is the background of debate behind the formularies, and a knowledge of that could well indicate that Haw's interpretation of them does not do justice to the wide divergences in Anglican opinion.

The second book, A. R. Winnett, *Divorce and Remarriage in Anglicanism*,[59] gives much of the information which Haw overlooks: he examines not only the formularies but, much more fully than Haw, the debates underlying them. Winnett documents the opinions of various influential bishops, and demonstrates that alongside the indissolubilist position which many Anglicans held, as Haw rightly notes, the 'non-indissolubilist' view deriving from the Continental Reformers has been strongly held by many Anglican leaders throughout the course of Anglican history. In fact, says Winnett in summary,[60] the Church of England has been 'acutely divided' on the issue from the time of the Reformation onwards.

The failure of the *Reformatio Legum* to become law prevented the Church of England from adopting the practice of the Reformed Churches on the continent, and the Canons of 1604 expressly disallowed divorce *a vinculo*. Nevertheless a large body of Anglican divines held that the teaching of our Lord in St Matthew allowed the dissolution of the marriage-bond for adultery.[61]

In the seventeenth century, Winnett argues[62] there was an almost equal division between the indissolubilist and non-indissolubilist views among Anglican divines.[63] In the eighteenth century the 'non-indissolubilist' view came to prevail,[64] and Winnett notes that 'no protest was made by the Church against the remarriage of those who had procured a divorce by Act of Parliament'.[65]

It was, however, primarily the Divorce Bill of 1857 which brought the question of divorce and remarriage into the fore-front of ecclesiastical debate in the most significant way since the Reformation, and we have in Chapter 1 explored in more detail Anglican debates since then. But we must now go back to the beginning to find our bearings with the English Reformers, and look specifically at the Prayer Book and at Canon Law.

The essentials of the Prayer Book service of 1662 are un-changed since the *Forme of Solemnizacion of Matrimonie* of 1549 (apart from spelling, and the giving of gold and silver with the ring), and though the 1549 service drew heavily on the Sarum Manual and to some extent on Hermann's *Consultatio*, we can be sure that the 1549, and 1552, service books reflected Cranmer's views at that time. Both the words of the pro-nouncement 'Those whome god hath ioyned together: let no man put a sundre', and the wording of the post-matrimonial prayer: 'and, knitting them together, diddest teache that it should neuer be lawful to put a sondre those, whome thou by matrimonie haddeste made one', declare the divine intention that marriage should be permanent, and should not be dissolved. On that point, as we have seen, the Roman tradition and the Continental Reformers were agreed, and there can be little doubt that Peter Martyr, for example, would have approved of such wording in the wedding service.

The question remains, however, as to Cranmer's attitude to divorce, and as we saw in discussing Martyr, it is perfectly

possible – indeed Martyr would have argued Scripturally
necessary – to affirm both the divine intention for the permanence of marriage, and yet allow for the lawfulness of
divorce as a grievous departure from that intention, in some
circumstances. Did Cranmer and the other English Reformers
share Martyr's view on this? For an answer, we must look at the
Reformatio Legum Ecclesiasticarum, a collection of proposed
revised Canons finalized in 1553. Twenty years earlier, Henry
VIII had ordered a review of Canon Law, but ruled that in the
meantime the validity of the old medieval canon law be provisionally extended. Under Edward VI a commission was set up
to reframe ecclesiastical law, and the original thirty-two
appointed a sub-committee of eight to draft the Code, among
them Archbishop Cranmer, and Peter Martyr, by then Professor of Theology at Oxford. There can be little doubt that a
good part of the work 'was done by Cranmer personally'.[66]
However, it never became law. When in the March of 1553
Cranmer would have had the scheme laid before Parliament,
Northumberland 'rudely bade him stick to his clerical functions'.[67] Within four months, Edward VI had died, there was
once more a Roman Catholic monarch, and the *Reformatio*
'disappeared into the pigeon holes'. It was eventually published
by Foxe in 1571. Despite its failure to become law, however, the
Reformatio affords a clear insight into the way Cranmer and,
at the very least, the great majority of the commission of
thirty-two persons who were appointed to prepare it, approached
the question of divorce. Its provisions included the severing of
the marriage *vinculum* for adultery, malicious desertion,
prolonged absence without news, attempts against the partner's
life, and cruelty. It prescribes severe punishment for adultery,
but enacts that the innocent partner is permitted to remarry
(quoting the Matthean exceptive clause as authority). In other
words it reflects the views of many Continental Protestants
(going even further than Martyr seems to in some cases), and
gives us evidence that Cranmer and the other English Reformers
of the time did not hold to the absolute indissolubility of the

marriage bond as upheld by medieval canon law. Joyce's summary seems the most adequate:

> It seems altogether unreasonable to suppose that the provisions on divorce merely reflect the foreign influences which at the moment swayed Cranmer's mind on that subject, and that so far as the English Reformers were concerned, it had no solid support behind it.[68]

> The English Reformers were of the same mind as their Continental brethren on this subject, but owing to the course which events took in this country, divorce failed to receive legal sanction.[69]

This conclusion is supported by the known views of other English Reformers. Tyndale, for example, had allowed freedom to the husband if the wife 'committed fornication', and the right of divorce and remarriage after desertion.[70]

Later Bishop Hooper of Gloucester and Worcester wrote that 'Christ putteth only one cause of divorcement for fornication' and this 'breaketh the knot of matrimony'[71] (so that the marriage bond once so broken and violated cannot be restored – a view that was described in a letter of John Ab Ulmis to Henry Bullinger in 1550 as 'too harsh and extreme').[72]

Among the charges brought against Hooper in January 1555 were that he 'had maintained and taught that married persons in the case of adultery, may by the word of God and his authority and by the ministry of the magistrates, be wholly separated from the bond of matrimony and divorced from one another'.[73]

Finally, we note that Cranmer's own Chaplain, Thomas Becon, allows divorce with liberty of remarriage on the grounds of adultery and persistent unbelief.[74]

It is from the perspective of the *Reformatio Legum* that we must assess the Canons of 1603. As we have noted, Henry VIII had left the ecclesiastical laws provisionally unaltered, pending their reform. These canons recognized divorce *a mensa et thoro* alone, and no divorce *a vinculo* was authorized for any cause. The death of Edward and the accession of Mary had involved

the failure of the *Reformatio* to become law, and in the un-
settled years in the latter half of the sixteenth century there
appears to have been considerable difference of opinion among
Anglican divines on the issue of divorce. In actual practice,
Joyce notes 'from the days of Edward VI to those of James I,
divorce and remarriage were extremely prevalent',[75] although
the weight of evidence seems to be against the view that the
Reformatio Legum ever governed the official practice of the
Church of England at that time. When the Canons of 1603
were formulated, it appears that it was the need for disciplinary
precaution in the light of frequent remarriage, rather than the
belief in the inherent indissolubility of the marriage bond, that
led to the continuation of medieval recognition only of divorce *a
mensa et thoro*, and of the refusal of the right of remarriage
under Church law. Canon 105 insists on evidence from witnesses
other than the partners in causes for separation. Canon 106
requires that all sentences for separation or annulment be given
in open court. Canon 107 requires a 'caution and restraint'
that parties so separated shall live 'chastely and continently',
neither shall they, during each other's life, contract matrimony
with any other person.

Both Joyce[76] and much more fully Winnett, document the
position from the end of the sixteenth century: 'The Church of
England officially committed to the old standards of law and
practice concerning marriage, but side by side with this the
opinion held by many influential Churchmen that adultery
dissolved the marriage bond and that the innocent husband was
free to remarry, an opinion which in a number of instances
found expression in practice' (by special Acts of Parliament).[77]

That division of opinion on the question of absolute indissolubility has been characteristic of Anglican history ever
since.[78] Indeed, the Lambeth Conference of 1888 expressly
noted that division. In particular, Resolution 4(a) reads

That, inasmuch as our Lord's words expressly forbid Divorce
except in the case of fornication or adultery, The Christian

Church cannot recognize Divorce in any other than the excepted case . . .

and (c): That recognizing the fact that there always has been a difference of opinion in the Church on the question whether our Lord meant to forbid marriage to the innocent party in a divorce for adultery, the Conference recommends that the Clergy should not be instructed to refuse the Sacraments or other privileges of the Church to those who, under civil sanction, are thus married.[79]

Those Resolutions, uncertain as they are, broke thirty years of almost complete silence from the episcopate since the Divorce Bill of 1857 had forced the question into the forefront of Christian thinking in the Church of England. That Bill had had an uncertain ride through Parliament, but when finally enacted made statutory provision for the first time for the dissolution of marriage on grounds of adultery, with right of remarriage. From then on the law of the land and the law of the Church as expressed in Canons 105-107 were at variance.

With this history, it is not suprising that the present Church of England betrays divergences of opinion. It is also clear that in the matter of divorce discipline and the refusal of any remarriage, the Church of England's position is more severe than that of any other Church. No branch of the Christian Church (except the modern Church of England) said Bishop Kirk in 1933, 'has been without some recognized loophole or safety valve'.[80] The Church of England stands alone 'in possessing no recognized safety valve for "hard cases" in matrimony'.[81] Whereas the Churches of the East and the Reformers allowed divorce, the Church of Rome (as we shall note further in a later chapter) established procedures for marriage-annulment.

A further point of importance which must not be overlooked is that much of the thinking of the Church is expressed in terms of law and discipline: the 'law' for marriage, the 'grounds' of divorce. Important as these are, they concern the external and institutional side of marriage. The meaning of the 'internal' covenant nature of marriage as a bond of personal fidelity, as we shall expound in the next chapter, must not ever be simply identified with its legal, institutional and ecclesiastical framework. It is to the biblical description of marriage as covenant that we now turn our attention.

SUMMARY OF CHAPTER 2

1 It appears that evidence from the early Fathers may be capable of differences of interpretation; the majority view is that (generally at least) the early Church did not normally permit divorce with remarriage.

2 Augustine grounded the indissolubility of marriage in the nature of the 'sacramental bond', understood as a bond of moral obligation and sacred sign.

3 The Eastern Churches have always allowed divorce with right of remarriage for a variety of causes.

4 The Church of Rome has held firmly to the law of absolute indissolubility, but since Vatican II there has been some pressure for the Church to recognize divorce and permit remarriage in certain circumstances.

5 The Continental Reformers sought to hold together the two principles of the divine law for the permanence of marriage, and the permissibility of divorce with right of remarriage as an exception in certain circumstances.

6 Archbishop Cranmer's attitude closely resembled that of Peter Martyr. The *Reformatio Legum Ecclesiasticarum*, Cranmer's proposed revised Canon Law which never reached Statute, permitted divorce with right of remarriage for adultery, malicious desertion, prolonged absence without news, attempts against the partner's life, cruelty.

7 Since the Reformation there has been a continual tension and debate between the 'indissolubilist' and the 'non-indissolubilist' traditions within the Church of England.

REFERENCES TO CHAPTER 2

1 O. D. Watkins, *Holy Matrimony* (1895); G. H. Joyce, *Christian Marriage* (Sheed and Ward, 1948)[2]; A. R. Winnett, *Divorce and Remarriage in Anglicanism* (Macmillan, 1958) and *Divorce and the*

Church (A. R. Mowbray, 1968); E. Schillebeeckx, *Marriage* (Sheed and Ward, 1965).

2 Joyce, *op. cit.*, p. 305.

3 Charles Gore, *The Question of Divorce* (John Murray, 1911), p. 32f.

4 V. Pospishil, *Divorce and Remarriage: Towards a New Catholic Teaching* (Burns and Oates, 1967), p. 44.

5 *Op. cit.*, p. 49.

6 *Op. cit.*, p. 43.

7 H. Crouzel, *Irish Theological Quarterly, 38* (1971), p. 21f, and his subsequent book: *L'Eglise primitive face au divorce: Du premier au cinquième siècle.*

8 Crouzel, *op. cit.*, p. 41.

9 V. Pospishil, *ITQ, 38* (1971), p. 338f.

10 Cheslyn Jones (ed.), *For Better, For Worse* (CLA, 1977)[2], p. 30.

11 Pospishil, *op. cit.*, p. 50.

12 Joyce, *op. cit.*, p. 317.

13 e.g. *On the Grace of Christ and Of Original Sin* Pt II chs 39, 42. *On Marriage and Concupiscence* Bk, 1 chs 11, 19. *On the Good of Marriage* sec. 32. For much of what follows I am indebted to an unpublished paper by Paul Ramsey, *Augustine and 'the Presiding Mind'.*

14 *On the Good of Marriage*, sec. 32.

15 *On the Good of Marriage*, sec. 32.

16 *On Marriage and Concupiscence*, Bk 1, ch. 11

17 *Op. cit.*, p. 318.

18 On the question how *sacramentum* came to translate the Greek *musterion* see G. Kittel (ed.), *Theologisches Worterbuch zum neuen Testament*: E T (G. Bromily, ed.) *Theological Dictionary of the New Testament* (Eerdmans, 1964) Vol. IV p. 827.

19 Schillebeeckx, *Marriage*, p. 283.

20 *Ibid.*, p. 141.

21 Schillebeeckx himself views these concepts, the patristic view of indissolubility of marriage as moral obligation, and the scholastic view of indissolubility as of an ontological bond, as complementary and mutually implicit. He believes they are both rooted in Scripture (*ibid.*, p. 141). We shall need to examine this further in the next chapter.

22 So Derek Harrison, and the authorities quoted in 'The Remarriage of Divorcees in the Orthodox Church' in Cheslyn Jones (ed.), *For Better, For Worse*, p. 27ff.

23 Joyce, *op. cit.*, p. 362.
24 Harrison, *op. cit.*, p. 28.
25 Cf. A. M. Allchin, 'The Sacrament of Marriage in Eastern Christianity' in *Marriage, Divorce and the Church* (SPCK, 1971), p. 124.
26 e.g. the Councils of Verberies and Compiegne, and numerous *Penitentials* of the seventh century onwards; details are given in Watkins, *op. cit.*, pp. 387, 414f.
27 A. R. Winnett. *op.cit.*, p. 1.
28 The view that the marriage bond involving an unbeliever could be severed under certain conditions. This was based on an interpretation of 1 Cor. 7:15, and we shall need to examine this further in Chapter 4. Cf. also Joyce, *op. cit.*, p. 477ff.
29 Cf. Denis O'Callaghan, 'Theology and Divorce', *ITQ, 37/3* (1970), p. 210f.
30 Cf. Joyce, *op. cit.*, p. 390.
31 *The Canons and Decrees of the Sacred and Oecumenical Council of Trent*, tr. J. Waterworth, Session XXIV.
32 Pospishil, *op. cit.*, p. 54f.
33 *Christian Marriage*, CTS translation of *Casti Connubii* (my italics).
34 Walter M. Abbott, *The Documents of Vatican II*, p. 250ff.
35 *Ibid.*, p. 489.
36 Cf. Denis O'Callaghan, *ITQ, 37/3* (1970) p. 210f.
37 O'Callaghan, *op. cit.*, p. 210. (The 'Petrine Privilege' is the claimed power of the Pope to dissolve a 'non-sacramental' union which has broken down.)
38 i.e. that though, for all practical purposes, a Catholic is obliged in conscience to assent to the teaching, it does not preclude the possibility that such teaching could be changed.
39 Cf. also Denis O'Callaghan, 'Theology and Divorce', *ITQ, 37/3* (1970), p. 210f; J. Dominian. 'The Christian Response to Marital Breakdown', *Ampleforth Journal*, 73/1 (1968), pp. 3-13.
Cf. Appendix 6 in *Marriage, Divorce and the Church*, the Report of the Commission on the Christian Doctrine of Marriage (1971). W. Harrington, 'Jesus' Attitude towards Divorce', *ITQ, 37/3* (1970), p. 199f.
Cf. also J. P. Jossua O.P., 'The Fidelity of Love and the Indissolubility of Christian Marriage', *The Clergy Review*, LVI (March 1971).
C. E. Curran, *Catholic Moral Theology in Dialogue* (1972), pp.

40, 41, also refers to B. Vawter C.M., 'The Biblical Theology of Divorce', *Proc. of the Catholic Theological Society of America*, XXII (1967), p. 223ff; and to W. W. Bassett, 'Divorce and Remarriage: The Catholic Search for a Pastoral Reconciliation', *American Ecclesiastical Review*, CLXII (1970), p. 100ff, and R. A. McCormick S.J., 'Notes on Moral Theology', *Theological Studies*, *32* (1971), p. 107ff.

Cf. also R. A. McCormick 'Divorce – Remarriage' in *Theological Studies*, *36* (1975), p. 100f.

40 Cf. H. Thielicke, *The Ethics of Sex* (James Clarke ET 1964), p. 131ff, and refs quoted.

41 *The Babylonian Captivity*, *Narrationes in Cap. V.VI.VII S. Mattaei*, and *Sermon on the Conjugal Life*; cf. also A. R. Winnett, *op. cit.*, p. 6 and G. H. Joyce, *Christian Marriage*, p. 409ff.

42 *Comm. on the Harmony of the Evangelists*, tr. W. Pringle (Edinburgh 1845), II, p. 384; quoted in R. J. Ehrlich, 'The Indissolubility of Marriage as a Theological Problem', *SJT*, *23/3* (August 1970), p. 303. Ehrlich continues with a discussion of the Scottish Reformer John Knox, who in *First Book of Discipline* (1560) was even more forthright:

> Marriage once lawfully contracted, may not be dissolved at man's pleasure, as our Master Christ Jesus doth witness, unless adultery be committed; which, being sufficiently proven in presence of the Civil Magistrate, the innocent (if they so require) ought to be pronounced free, and the offender ought to suffer death as God hath commanded. If the Civil sword foolishly spare the life of the offender, yet may not the Church be negligent in their office, which is to excommunicate the wicked, and to repute them as dead members, and to pronounce the innocent party to be at freedom, be they never so honourable before the world. (Cf. Ehrlich, *op. cit.*, p. 303f.)

43 Joyce, *op. cit.*, p. 416.

44 M. Bucer, *De Regno Christi*. Chs. 15, 17, 19, 21–47 were translated as 'The Judgement of Martin Bucer touching Divorce' by John Milton in 1644 and are available in Milton's Prose Works.

45 In a letter to Henry Bullinger, dated 8 June 1550, John Burcher writes: 'Bucer is more than licentious on the subject of marriage. I heard him once disputing at table upon the question, when he asserted that a divorce should be allowed for any reason, however trifling; so that he is considered, not without cause, by our

Bishop of Winchester as the author of the book published in defence of the Landgrave.' The latter reference is to the marriage of Philip of Hess, who took a second wife with the knowledge and apparent lack of disapproval of Luther, Melanchthon and Bucer.

46 For example the *Parker Society* volumes, 3 *Zur.* p. 416, 3 *Zur.* p. 404.
47 *Op. cit.*, p. 418.
48 *Op. cit.*, p. 422.
49 *Op. cit.*, p. 423, arguing against polygamy.
50 *Op. cit.*, p. 457.
51 *Op. cit.*, p. 458.
52 *Ibid.*
53 *Ibid.*
54 *Ibid.*
55 R. Haw, *The State of Matrimony* (SPCK, 1952).
56 *Ibid.*, p. 179.
57 *Ibid.*, p. 180.
58 *Ibid.*, p. 181.
59 *Op. cit.*
60 *Ibid.*, p. vii.
61 Winnett, *op. cit.*, p. vii.
62 *Ibid.*, p. 6of.
63 *Ibid.*, p. vii.
64 *Ibid.*, p. 118f.
65 *Ibid.*, p. vii.
66 Philip Hughes, *The Reformation in England* (Burns and Oates, 1963)[5], p. 129; Reformation historians seem agreed on this point; cf. also A. G. Dickens, *The English Reformation* (Fontana ed. 1967), p. 344 in which he speaks of 'Cranmer's *Reformatio Legum Ecclesiasticarum*'; cf. also *The Canon Law of the Church of England*, Report of the Archbishops Commission (1947), p. 46: 'The new code reached the stage of being revised by Archbishop Cranmer.'

Haw, however, argues that since the *Reformatio*'s recommendations are substantially the same as Peter Martyr's, the work must largely have been Martyr's and not Cranmer's (whom he believes from the Prayer Book service to have held an indissolubilist position). Thus Haw regards the *Reformatio* as the high water mark of Continental Protestant influence in the Church of England, from which the Church was in fact preserved by the failure of the *Reformatio* to become law.

67 P. Hughes, *op. cit.*, p. 129.

68 Joyce, *op. cit.*, p. 420.
69 *Ibid.*, p. 418.
70 *Parker Soc.* volume 2 *Tyn.* pp. 51, 54.
71 *Hoop.* I, p. 381.
72 3 *Zur.* p. 416.
73 2 *Hoop.* xxiii.
74 Cf. e.g. 3 *Bec.* p. 532; and *The Book of Matrimony* in *Works* pt. 1. (1564).
75 Joyce, *op. cit.*, p. 421.
76 *Op. cit.*, p. 422f.
77 Winnett, *op. cit.*, p. 55.
78 The main sections of Winnett *Divorce and Remarriage in Anglicanism* document the debate between Anglican 'indissolubilists' and 'non-indissolubilists'.
79 *The Six Lambeth Conferences*, p. 119f.
80 K. E. Kirk, *Marriage and Divorce* (Hodder and Stoughton, 1948)[2], p. 34.
81 *Ibid.*, p. 106.

CHAPTER 3

The Marriage Covenant

Karl Barth is surely right in expounding 'covenant fidelity' as the inner meaning and purpose of our creation as human beings in the divine image, and the whole of the created order as the external framework for, and condition of the possibility of keeping covenant.[1] From early Genesis through God's dealings with Abraham, at Sinai, with David, through the prophets and in clearest focus in the New Covenant in Christ, God's covenant of grace with his people forms the framework by which his people's lives are to be ordered.[2] By covenant is meant an agreement between two parties based on promise, which includes these four elements: first, an undertaking of committed faithfulness made by one party to the other (or by each to the other); secondly, the acceptance of that undertaking by the other party; thirdly, public knowledge of such an undertaking and its acceptance; and fourthly, the growth of a personal relationship based on and expressive of such a commitment.

God's covenant of grace with his people is made first by the initiative of his gracious promise and its associated requirement: 'I will be your God, you shall be my people', and then by his people's acceptance of his undertaking to be their God in their response of obedient love to him. The public nature of such promise and response was often declared by the giving of a covenant sign.[3] Covenant theology is thus a theology of personal pronouns: 'I will . . . you shall . . .' The covenant relationship is the life of faithful response to God's initiative and promise and continuing gift of faithful love.

As Paul Ramsey says, 'the conscious acceptance of covenant responsibilities is the inner meaning of even the "natural" or systemic relations into which we are born and of the institutional relations or roles we enter by choice, while this fabric provides the external framework for human fulfilment in explicit covenants among men'.[4]

If all human relations can be expressed in covenant terms, this is particularly true of man-woman relationships, and of the ultimate expression of the man-woman relationship in marriage. Indeed the fundamental biblical description of marriage is given in covenant terms, and the interchange of analogies by which human marriage is used to describe's God's covenant relationship with his people, and by which God's relationship with his people, or Christ's with his Church, is used to provide a pattern for human marriage, can be traced through both Old and New Testaments.

We shall first explore this interchange of analogies, and then seek to expound in more detail the meaning of human marriage as covenant, and the way in which the covenant framework holds together the sexual and familial, personal and social, aspects of marriage. We cannot, clearly, offer here a complete exposition of the biblical material on the meaning and obligations of married life, but select that which particularly helps in setting the context for our discussion in the following chapters of the problems of divorce and remarriage.

Marriage as Covenant

There are few specific references to marriage as a covenant in the Old Testament. Proverbs 2:17 speaks of human marriage in a covenant context, although the reference there is probably primarily to God's covenant with Israel including the obligations of the seventh commandment. Malachi 2:14 is more explicit: 'The Lord was witness to the covenant between you and the wife of your youth ...' The implicit link between human marriage and God's covenant with his people, however, is very widely used. Frequently the covenant of grace between God and his people is expressed in human marriage terms. Human married life, its uncertainties as well as its certainties, its joys and its hard times, love and the temptations to infidelity, all this (to borrow Schillebeeckx's phrase) 'formed the prism' through which the prophets proclaimed the saving covenant of God with his people: human marriage became the means of revealing the meaning of covenant. Also, by 'reciprocal illumination', by revealing his covenant through the medium of human marriage, God simultaneously revealed a meaning in human marriage which the people had hitherto not fully apprehended.[5]

It was the prophet Hosea (especially in Chapters 1-3) who first (c. 725 BC) expounded God's covenant of grace by reference to the human reality of marriage. Hosea's personal marriage to Gomer, a harlot (who had taken part in Baal fertility rites), and her subsequent departure to 'her lovers' (2:5), is used as a picture of Israel's unfaithfulness to God. Since the days of Solomon the nation had never been as rich or as secure politically – nor as lawless (4:6), as immoral (4:10) or as pagan (3:1). They had, like Hosea's wife (2:8) become blind to the love of God to them (2:13). All Gomer had the right to expect from Hosea – all faithless Israel had the right to expect from God – was the judgement of divorce.[6] But then (3:1) the second theme of the prophecy is introduced:

> And the Lord said to me, 'Go again, love a woman who is beloved of a paramour and is an adulteress; even as the Lord loves the people of Israel, though they turn to other gods ...'

Hosea journeys to find his runaway wife, and pays the third party to whom she now belongs (3:2) to buy her back to himself. This second theme in Hosea's personal life story is used as a picture of the second theme of the prophet's message: that despite Israel's unfaithfulness to God, God's steadfast love and mercy remain constant, and a way is found for the relationship to be restored (cf. 2:18-23, etc.).

The book of Jeremiah, likewise, constantly refers to the images of marriage and infidelity to describe the covenant of grace, and the sin of covenant-breaking, between God's people and himself. Thus Israel's apostasy (Jer. 2:20f) is expressed in the language of divorce (3:1, 20). And yet, as with Hosea, Jeremiah's final word is of God's eternal love (31:3ff).

> The Lord has created a new thing on the earth: a woman protects a man (i.e. the wife shall return to her husband) (31:22).

To give a third example, Ezekiel uses the image of 'infidelity', the 'harlot', the 'adulteress' in his vivid descriptions of Jerusalem's 'marriage' with the Lord. In Chapter 16, for example, Jerusalem is depicted as God's bride: her birth (16:4), her growth to marriageable age (16:7), their betrothal and marriage (in covenant language) (16:8), and her infidelity and adultery (16:15-34) are traced out, and God's punishment for unfaithfulness is clear (16:40). Yet, even though the marriage covenant was broken (16:59), God will not forget his promise of love (16:60f).

In a final example from the prophets, Isaiah uses the marriage imagery, and here there is an even stronger indication that although divorce is real in God's punishment for Israel's unfaithfulness, the separation is not permanent, and the abandoned bride will be brought home. So (50:1), 'Thus says the Lord: "Where is your mother's bill of divorce, with which I put her away?"' and (54:6-8):

> For the Lord called you like a wife forsaken and grieved in spirit, like a wife of youth when she is cast off, says your God. For a brief moment I forsook you, but with great compassion I will gather you. In overflowing wrath for a moment I hid my face from you, but with everlasting love I will have compassion on you, says the Lord, your Redeemer.

The new 'marriage' continues the covenant obligations of the first. (It is noteworthy that this renewal in ch. 54 follows immediately on the work of the Servant of chs 42-53.)

This 'covenant of personal pronouns' by which it becomes true both of God's relationship to his people, and a husband's with his wife that 'either is the other's Mine',[7] is reflected in the theological comment of Genesis 2:24 on the narrative of the creation of Eve from Adam (2:18ff): 'Therefore a man leaves his father and his mother and cleaves to his wife, and they become one flesh.'

This Genesis verse is used in the words of Jesus reported by Matthew and Mark, and in the words of Paul in Ephesians 5, as the foundation for a doctrine of marriage. In Matt. 19 and Mark 10, Gen. 2:24 is coupled with a reference to the first creation narrative in Gen. 1:27. The marriage covenant (a man . . . his wife . . . one flesh) is thus set within the theological (if not the literary) context of the creation of man as male and female in the image of God.

In the Ephesian passage, the analogies are interchanged. Christ and his Church are pictured as bridegroom and bride, but the context in which this is set is the exposition of the obligations of human married life which is, says Paul, to be patterned on the relationship of Christ with his Church. It is of the living bond of committed love between Christ and the Church that Paul uses the language of 'one flesh'. (Indeed, some manuscripts read v.30: 'We are members of his body, of his flesh and of his bones', words that though omitted in the best texts, are none the less congruent with the allusions to Gen. 2:24 in Eph. 5:31 – see discussion below.) The covenant language implicit in the pronouns of Gen. 2, is thus made explicit in Eph. 5. This covenant concept is integrally related to God's action and intention in creation.

This needs to be kept foremost in mind when we come to such questions as the 'purpose of marriage'. Whereas both Reformed and Catholic theologies have usually answered the question as to the purpose of marriage in terms such as the following (although differing in order of priority): the procreation of children, the mutual help and comfort of husband and wife for each other, the 'prevention of unchastity'[8] – and whereas all this may well be true – there is a prior answer to be given. The primary purpose of marriage is to be found in the acceptance of God's will that the covenant relationship of man and wife, both made in the image of God, shall be an image of his covenant relationship with his people. Barth goes further[9] in his description of the duality of maleness and femaleness in creation, in their differentiation and relationship, as part of the meaning of the 'image of God' itself (Gen. 1.27). Whether or not this particular exegesis is correct,[10] the exposition of marriage in terms of covenant is well expressed by Ehrlich (following Barth) when he says

> Marriage, which is the supreme expression of the togetherness of male and female in differentiation and relationship, (reflects the image of God and) represents the covenant by which God has bound himself to his people, his church, to man.[11]

We can now begin to identify some of the more important implications for marriage of the use of covenant terminology, and we take as our starting point an exposition of this theme by G. R. Dunstan.[12] He suggests five marks of comparison between God's covenant with his people and human marriage. The first is an *initiative of love* inviting a response, and so creating a relationship.[13] Secondly, as God's covenant of grace is made sure by oath, so the essence of the marriage covenant is the *vow of consent*, the vow 'guarding the union against the fitfulness of the emotional bond, and against the destructiveness, indeed, of emotional power'.[14] Thirdly, covenant conditions are expressed in commandments from God to men. These are paralleled in marriage by covenant *obligations of faithfulness* (which we discuss more fully below). The fourth mark of God's covenant, says Dunstan, is the *promise of blessing* to those who remain faithful to their covenant obligations. Here Dunstan comments: 'The great word of Genesis that a man shall cleave unto his wife and they shall become one flesh, is at once command and promise. It is a command: press on to that unity for the sake of your perfection; see that you fall not out by the way;

do not forsake the covenant yourself; and if the other does, remember God in Christ, faithful to his bride the Church, and so forgive, to the uttermost. This is the command of God. And the promise is that this, the impossible is possible. The two do become one, and "signify", or exemplify to the world "the mystical union that is betwixt Christ and his Church". What God commands he also gives.'[15] The fifth mark of covenant is *sacrifice*. In both testaments, the covenant of God with his people is secured by the laying down of life in death. In marriage, too, there is death: death to the dependence of childhood; death to bachelor or spinster freedoms and certain rights of self-determination; death to self as a whole, 'in order to rise to a wholeness of a new sort with the spouse'.[16]

In these comparisons, Professor Dunstan is opening up ways of understanding how the human marriage covenant can be patterned on the covenant of God, and so become a demonstration and illustration to the world of what that latter relationship means and entails. That is the primary purpose of marriage, as the Bible discloses its meaning to us. It thus becomes one of the primary tasks of the Christian Church to enable and foster the growth of such relationships which in marriage can and do declare the meaning and character of God's covenant relationship with his people.

We move now from these marks of comparison between divine and human covenants to a further discussion of the meaning of the human marriage covenant itself. It is convenient to return, as the heading for the following sections, to that 'great text of Genesis' which comes as a theological comment from the narrator after the description of the creation of woman out of the flesh of man:

> Therefore a man leaves his father and his mother and cleaves to his wife, and they become one flesh (2:24).

Here are the three strands from which a human marriage covenant is made: 'leaving', 'cleaving', 'one flesh'.

In this rich simplicity, the narrator is giving us hints towards his understanding of several facts of life,[17] including human sexuality, the foundational importance of the family, the central concept of covenant fidelity, and the fact that covenant relationships belong within an institutional framework. We shall use this text as a peg and pointer, in our discussion of these themes as they occur here and elsewhere in the Bible. It will be convenient to reverse the Genesis order.

(i) 'One flesh': the question of human sexuality

What is the meaning of the powerful drive of the sexes to each other? Or, as von Rad asks in his commentary on Genesis,

> Whence comes this love 'strong as death' (Song. 8.6), and stronger than the tie to one's parents, whence this inner clinging to each other, this drive towards each other which does not rest until it again becomes one flesh in the child?

He answers:

> It comes from the fact that God took woman from man, that they actually were originally *one* flesh. Therefore they must come together again and thus by destiny belong to each other. The recognition of this narrative as aetiological is theologically important. Its point of departure, the thing to be explained, is for the narrator something in existence, present, and not something 'paradisal' and thus lost![18]

Whether or not we need go as far as von Rad in the androgyne concept, it is clear that Gen. 2:24 is answering a question. The whole second creation story of which this verse is the climax, introduces us to the fact that our life on earth is (to use Smedes's expression) 'body-life'.[19] It is in the woman (and not anywhere else in creation) that Adam finds the fulfilment of the needs of his whole life – his 'body-life'. 'This at last is bone of my bone and flesh of my flesh; she shall be called woman' (*Ishshah*). Here are now *Ish* and *Ishshah* together as 'body-persons'. Now the man knew what it was to be male 'for he saw himself in relation to one (the woman) who was the same as he, but with the crucial difference'.[20] Male and female know themselves in relation to each other, because they are made for each other. In the reasoning of the Genesis writer, this is the deep origin of the powerful drive of the sexes to come together.

It is when we then remember that the theological context of Gen. 2:24 is Gen. 1:27 (so we are taught by the words of Jesus in Matt. 19 and Mark 10), that it is possible to appreciate Barth's point that sexuality is part of the meaning of the divine image.[21] If human sexuality is the human drive towards personal communion ('Beyond the glandular impulse the human sexual urge is always towards another person'[22]) then Barth's emphasis is right to the extent at least that human sexuality is a deep dimension of the God-like in us. Christian theology has not traditionally been marked by the emphasis that sexuality is, at all levels, the deeply human drive towards discovering what personal relationship means at its most intimate, and that sexual intercourse is the physical climax of personal union between a man and a woman. However, sexual passion is explicitly part of the goodness of the relationship between bride and groom in the Song of Songs, and the young man warned against the blandishments of the immoral woman (in Proverbs 5:3f) is none the less exhorted (vv. 18-19) to enjoy the sexual pleasures of the embrace of his wife. Is not such delight also implicit in the words of Adam: 'This *at last* is bone of my bone and flesh of my flesh'?[23]

This is not to say, of course, that a person cannot be a whole person without sexual intercourse. There can be personal communion without sexual intercourse, just as there can be sex-union without relating as persons. As Smedes puts it[24], 'Although virgins do not experience the climax of sexual-personal existence, they can experience personal wholeness by giving themselves to other persons without physical sex. Through a life of self-giving – which is at the heart of sexual union – they become whole persons. They capture the essence without the usual form.'

It is thus within the context of the nature and function of human sexuality – the reflection of the covenant of God in interpersonal encounter – that the marriage covenant is set. After describing the fact of creation (1:27), and the origin of human sexuality (2:18f), the narrator of Gen. 2:24 then establishes the meaning of marriage: an exclusive ('a man . . . his wife . . .'), permanent ('cleaves to . . .') interpersonal communion ('one flesh'). Marriage is the context in which such interpersonal male-female relations find their most complete expression; it is a life-partnership of self-giving love, by which God's covenant pattern for life can (increasingly in time) be expressed.

This is the way, therefore, that 'one flesh' must be understood: 'It signifies the coming into being of a unitary existence, a complete partnership of man and woman, which cannot therefore be broken up without damage to the partners in it' (Seebass).[25] 'One flesh' does not then in the first instance mean sexual intercourse, although in the marriage context[26] it includes it. In his detailed study of the meaning of 'one flesh' in *The Mystery of Love and Marriage*, Sherwin Bailey says that 'although the union in "one flesh" is a physical union established by sexual intercourse . . . it involves at the same time the whole being, and affects the personality at the deepest level. It is a union of the entire man with the entire woman.'[27] That is not to say, however, that every act of intercourse establishes this total 'one flesh' union.[28] It is possible to engage in genital contact without any personal intercommunion. Neither is 'one flesh' in this sense necessarily created by a wedding ceremony. Every marriage is not automatically or necessarily such a complete partnership. 'One flesh' is rather the promise of marriage which may be claimed. It is the meaning of marriage granted by God. His action in the total union of one man giving himself totally – in intention initially and increasingly as the covenant relationship deepens in time – to one woman, who gives herself totally in the same sense in response. This union is first established by and finds growing physical expression in sexual intercourse. It grows to be more and more in fact what it is in intention, as the relationship works out in time.[29]

This interpretation of 'one flesh' is consistent with the other Old Testament references to 'my bone and my flesh' which mean 'my blood relation, my kinsman'.[30] The primary reference of 'one flesh' in Gen. 2:24 is not therefore to sexual intercourse, but to the closest possible personal relationship. This interpretation, emphasizing the 'oneness' rather than the 'flesh', is supported by the two occurrences of the phrase in the New Testament Epistles.

In Ephesians 5:31-2, the context is the great mystery by which Christ is united to his Church. There is a sense in which the uniqueness of Christ is complemented by the 'oneness in relationship' in which he is joined to his Church, his body, his bride. And if 'one flesh' can describe *that* union, the total unity of Spirit, the intercommunion between the Head and the members, which finds expression both in terms of this world's environment and in that of the world to come, then 'one flesh' should be understood primarily in that sense in the husband-wife marriage union which Paul expounds in terms of Christ's relationship with his Church, and of which, in this world, sexual intercourse is the appropriate physical expression.[31]

In the second reference in the Epistles (1 Cor. 6:16-20), Paul seems to be referring to the problem that some Corinthian Christians were acting as though it did not matter to separate their sexual activities from their spiritual commitment to Christ. It is a reductionist sort of philosophy: 'The body is for sex, and sex for the body . . . and that is all' (as we might understand v.13). Paul's answer is that sexual intercourse in God's creation pattern (v.16b) is to be an expression of the totality of the person in commitment to the other, and that such splitting of the moral from the spiritual is abhorrent and utterly wrong. The whole body is the temple of the Holy Spirit, is a member of Christ; the whole body-personality is involved in the immoral behaviour. Whenever a man and a woman consent freely to engage in sexual relations, their intercourse makes them in some sense, 'one flesh'. Sherwin Bailey[32] here draws a distinction between two sharply contrasted states of 'one flesh':

(i) the authentic 'henosis' effected by intercourse following consent between a man and a woman who love one another and who act freely, deliberately and responsibly, and with the knowledge and approval of the community, and in so doing (whether they know it or not) conform to the Divine Law, (ii) the false, invalid (we might add 'caricature') 'one flesh', effected by casual or mercenary acts of fornication or by adultery – such as at Corinth. Or, as Smedes comments vividly on 1 Cor.: 6:

> There is no such thing as casual sex, no matter how casual people are about it. The Christian assaults reality in his night out at the brothel. He uses a woman and puts her back in a closet where she can be forgotten; but the reality is that he has put away a person with whom he has done something that was meant to inseparably join them.[33]

Sexual intercourse is meant to be the expression of 'one flesh' in its fullest sense: the total person in commitment to the other. So, says Paul to the Corinthians, stop acting as if it were not. Sherwin Bailey adds two further distinctions: (i)

> There are very many unions which appear to be valid, but which must properly be termed defective. These are the marriages which have no foundation in love – or which, because of sexual or physical maladjustment represent a level of personal relation which falls considerably below the ideal implied by 'one flesh'.

To this we add the comment that 'defective' is a better term than 'invalid'. A marriage which in all 'externals' is valid, but which lacks the inner meaning of the 'one flesh' bond, is better understood as a bad and defective marriage than as no marriage at all. (ii) Sherwin Bailey continues:

> There are cases, such as rape and the seduction of the young and feeble minded where it would be absurd to press the application of Paul's principle (viz. that even with the Corinthian harlot 'one flesh' of some description is created) . . . the mere occurrence of the sexual act without consent, desire or understanding cannot be held to make two persons one 'body'.[34]

We can now summarize from these passages concerning 'one

flesh', three norms for sexual moral behaviour (following the exposition of Smedes).[35] First, the sexuality of every person is meant to be integrated into the whole character and moral life of that person (a norm which is broken, as at Corinth, when physical sex is severed from the rest of a person's life). Secondly, the sexuality of every person is meant to be an urge towards and an expression of personal communion with another person (a norm which is broken when another person is used only as a sex-object; sex becomes a self-centred goal). Thirdly, the sexuality of every person is meant to move him towards a permanent heterosexual union of committed love (which is broken when a person is led into affairs that frustrate or ignore that possibility). All three norms belong together. In other words: the marriage covenant and sexual union belong together. Sexual intercourse thus has a *unitive* function within the marriage covenant: it is an expression of and a deepening of the 'one flesh'.

(ii) *'One flesh': the foundation of the family*

We return to the second 'fact of life' to which the Genesis narrative points. Genesis 2:24, as we have sought to illustrate, leads us to a meaning for sexual union within the marriage covenant. But it does more than this.

'A man leaves his father and mother and cleaves to his wife . . .' Some commentators take this as an echo of the system of matriarchy in which the woman was head of the family. U. Cassuto[36] does not think it is necessary to take the passage thus.

> The meaning of the verse is simply this: Whilst a man is single, he forms part of his father's family, but when he takes a wife, he founds a new family; so long as he is in his father's house, all his love is dedicated to his father and mother, but when he is married, his love for his wife transcends that for his parents.

If, from the personal point of view, marriage and human sexual union belong together, from the sociological point of view, marriage and the family belong together.[37] Further, if, as we have argued, the primary reference of 'one flesh' in Gen. 2:24 is personal, in social terms the establishment of a new family within which the 'one flesh' union of husband and wife can issue in the 'one flesh' of a child.[38] The nuclear family is a universal human institution,[39] and by linking the marriage covenant ('a man . . . his wife . . .') to the family ('leave . . . cleave . . .'), the narrator of Genesis is expressing the purpose of the family as the context in which children are brought up by (and not just biologically begotten by) their parents. This could be expressed another way by saying that the marriage and family interrelationship of Gen. 2:24 is the creation pattern in which the creation command of 1:27-8 ('male and female he created them . . . Be fruitful and multiply . . .') is intended to be fulfilled.

While, therefore, a primary purpose of human sexual relationship is the *unitive* purpose of expressing and deepening personal communion between the marriage partners, a further purpose of human sexuality is the *procreative* purpose of building a family. As Paul Ramsey so cogently argues,[40] these unitive and procreative aspects of sexual union belong together within the marriage covenant. It is no accident, therefore, that God's covenant with his people is founded in the calling of Abraham to be the father of a family (Gen. 17:2), and that all human family life is said to derive its meaning, purpose, and sustaining love from the Fatherhood of God (Eph. 3:14ff). The marriage covenant (and its central heart, 'one flesh') combines the context in which human sexuality finds its fulfilment and that in which human family life finds its foundation.

(iii) 'Cleaving': the central concept of covenant-fidelity

Thirdly, the use of the word 'cleave' in Gen. 2:24, reflects the understanding of the marriage relationship as one of permanent and committed faithfulness. 'Cleaving' is a word which occurs also in non-sexual contexts, frequently meaning to join to someone in a permanent way, as Ruth 'clave unto' Naomi (Ruth 1:14, *Authorized Version*) and the men of Judah 'clave unto their king' (2 Sam. 20:2). Its use in 1 Esdras 4:20 ('A man leaves his own father, who brought him up, and his own country, and cleaves to his wife') shows that in the marriage context it has a wider reference than the sexual to include the whole relationship. It is one of the words used in the contexts of God's covenant with his people, urging on the people the importance of committed faithfulness in response to God's grace. Thus Deut. 10:20 reads 'You shall fear the Lord your God; you shall serve him and cleave to him . . .' – part of the meaning of obedience to the God of the Sinai covenant (20:1off). Likewise 'cleave to the Lord your God' is part of the covenant obligations referred to in Josh. 22:5 and 23:8.[41]

The sense of permanent committed faithfulness to which this word points seems to be the central concept which more than any other holds together all the inner meanings (to which Professor Dunstan referred) of the covenant relationship secured by a vow, and now lived by self-sacrificing love. Words like 'steadfast love', 'faithfulness' frequently describe the relationship of the covenant God with his people: 'know therefore that the Lord your God is God, the faithful God who keeps covenant and steadfast love with those who love him and keep his commandments . . .' (Deut. 7:9, etc.); these are words which in the marriage context describe the essential dimension of self-giving love expressed between the covenant partners. The Old English word for such a quality in marriage is *troth*. On this Olthuis comments that *troth*

Captures the nuances of trust, reliability, stability, scrupulousness, ingenuousness, authenticity, integrity and fidelity . . .

The call to troth is a unique dimension of the call to be human, the call to love God and our neighbour. God's call to love is many sided; we are to execute our responsibilities with style, taste, dignity and conviction; we are to take care of ourselves and the rest of creation with sensitivity and concern. God's call to be human also means that we must answer the invitation to troth. By nature man responds to this call; he cannot escape it. In part, humanity means pledging troth or breaking troth, counting on others or distrusting them, keeping one's word or playing fast and loose with one's promises . . .

Then in the context of marriage:

If men and women respond positively to the troth call, their lives acquire new depth and meaning. People can count on each other, and counting on one another leads to understanding and sharing, to integrity, genuineness and commitment . . .

Troth is the moral expression of love.[42]

The centre of the meaning of marriage (not what it is *for*, nor how it is made, but what it *means*) is the expression of a bond of moral troth (that is, covenant faithfulness) in which two people marry each other before God, and pledge to each other loyalty, trust, devotion and reliability. The word 'fidelity' now can have a very negative ring to it. It too often merely amounts to 'putting a leash on lust'.[43] But troth-fidelity, covenant-faithfulness, is primarily an affirmation. The negative cast of the seventh commandment 'Thou shalt not commit adultery' has a positive base, 'You shall be faithful', and this means faithfulness in all the many dimensions which marriage covers. The model of creative, covenant faithfulness seen in the steadfast love and faithfulness of God, indicates that faithfulness in marriage can and should be something positive, creative and dynamic: much more than the avoidance of adultery. Within a marriage, covenant faithfulness will mean at least the following four things (following Smedes).[44]

(a) Faithfulness to a vow

The vow says that life has an intentional side to it: life is sustained by willing choice. Faithfulness to the marriage vow is not essentially (what it can sometimes become, or be forced to become) a cold and dogged determination to 'stick it out'. Faithfulness to a vow is a function of the will: it is an act of intention that 'for better for worse', the partners will not let circumstances or 'fate' determine the future of their relationship. As O'Donovan writes:

> Marriage . . . *contains* the sufferings that are likely to arise in the
> course of a long relationship by forging from the joy and delight
> which marks the beginning of it, a bond of loyalty which will hold
> firm in the face of them.[45]

The vow points to the fact that a marriage is built on more
than eros; faithfulness to a vow can mean that, even in the
troubled times when eros has apparently burnt out, it can –
with the right will – be revived.

(b) Faithfulness to a calling

This parallels what Dunstan called 'obligation'. Against the
romantic view in which marriage is seen only as an intimate
relationship chosen for personal fulfilment, and against the
'institutional' view that marriage is merely a social status by
which two people are legally bound together, we need to revive
the sense that marriage is a calling to be lived before God, open
to the resources of his grace and forgiveness, and his will for the
future. This rescues marriage from static and restrictive legal
concepts, and opens it to the possibility of future growth and
deeper fulfilment. Smedes quotes Bonhoeffer's sermon prepared
for a wedding in which he accepts that marriage is a status, but
turns it towards the sense of vocation:

> Marriage is more than your love for each other. It has a higher
> dignity and power, for it is God's holy ordinance . . . In your love
> you see only the heaven of your happiness, but in marriage you
> are placed at a post of responsibility towards the world and man-
> kind. Your love is your own private possession, but marriage is
> something more than personal – it is a status, an office . . . that
> joins you together in the sight of God and man.

(c) Faithfulness to a person

If troth is the moral expression of love, it is essentially person-
directed; when faithfulness becomes function-based, it becomes
less than moral. Thus to be faithful in marriage because of
security or prestige, for the sake only of sexual release or only
for the sake of the children, is to cast faithfulness in a negative

light, as a function-based duty. 'Positive fidelity is first of all a dedication to the freedom, maturity and growth of the other *person*.'[46]

(d) Faithfulness to a relationship

Whereas the marriage partnership finds room for individual growth, comments Smedes under this heading, 'at the beating heart of any marriage is the delicate, fragile, often painful but potentially joyful relationship of two persons face to face in personal encounter'.[47] It is an 'obligation to keep the door open to future possibilities of better personal relationships'.

If the marriage covenant implies faithfulness in such dimensions, it implies also that such faithfulness can only be expressed within a permanent and lifelong structure. If marriage is not considered a permanent trust for life, 'it is in a permanent crisis'. If the 'freedom to leave' is regarded as a real option, it becomes a 'spectre which haunts the marriage'.[48] Consequently there is not the freedom to develop the sort of marriage relationship which we have characterized by covenant faithfulness, except within the structure of a permanent and lifelong relationship of committed love.

(iv) *'Leaving father and mother': the 'institutional' framework of covenant*

The at first sight anachronistic phrase in Gen. 2:24 'leave father and mother', points – we have suggested – to the establishment by marriage of a new family unit. It serves as a reminder that emotional and psychological security within a marriage must presuppose an emotional as well as a physical separation from 'father and mother'. (In a sense this is the first step in making the marriage. The Genesis order: 'leaving' . . . 'cleaving' . . . 'one flesh' is the order in which the marriage covenant is made; I have reversed that order in discussion to focus primarily on the meaning of the covenant relationship.) It serves also as a pointer to the fact that the marriage relationship of 'cleaving' and 'becoming one flesh', on which the new family unit depends, is established in a publicly known way. It is presupposed throughout both Old and New Testaments that marriage is a publicly acknowledged relationship.[49]

One of the marks of covenant, whether of God with his people, or of husband with his wife, is its public nature. There is no question that this particular man who has left father and mother is now married to this particular woman, and not another.

In other words, while the central 'inner' meaning of the marriage covenant is expressed by the committed permanent 'cleaving' and the total self-giving of one partner to the other in 'one flesh', the covenant concept also includes the sense of public recognition and accountability: the 'external' framework of the covenant relationship is a certain sort of social institution.

We need to clarify at this point what is meant by marriage as 'institution'. The Book of Common Prayer speaks of marriage as 'instituted by God in the time of man's innocency', and here the reference is to the creation pattern in which God intended sexual and family life to be arranged, namely around committed permanent partnerships of faithful love. Marriage is thus a 'natural' institution, and not a 'conventional' institution (which is a man-made social structure for a particular purpose). O'Donovan values the description of this aspect of marriage as 'institution' (rather than merely 'contract'), because the term makes clear that within marriage one is subject to an 'order of necessity'. But marriage, he goes on, is not an institution in the same sense that, say, the University of Toronto is an institution. If the latter 'conventional' institution ceases to fulfil the purposes of its founders it may be dissolved. 'Marriage is not an institution of that kind. Nobody invented it, and nobody can abolish it. It is a "natural" institution as opposed to a "conventional" one. Of course each society surrounds marriage with its own conventional rituals and forms; but marriage itself, the principle of lifelong monogamy, is not conventional . . . It belongs to the creative gift of God that precedes all human purposes and plans. The only answer to the question "Why marriage?" is that God has made it so.'[50]

This is not, of course, to deny the importance of social, legal and ecclesiastical structures; on the contrary, such social frameworks can themselves act as supports for the divine pattern for marriage and as barriers without which personal relationships would often be that much harder to maintain.

Whatever particular social, legal or ecclesiastical form or ceremony is involved in any particular society, however, the divine pattern for marriage includes both the internal personal commitments and the external public accountability inherent in the meaning of covenant.

What, then, 'makes a marriage'?

The marriage covenant, as we have sought to understand it from the biblical perspective, includes the following features:

Its central theme is the commitment of a man and a woman to each other into an exclusive relationship of moral 'troth' which is intended to be permanent, and to be patterned on and in its turn display the meaning and character of God's relationship with his people, Christ's with his Church. The marriage relationship is intended to be – and increasingly to become – the 'one flesh' union of total love-commitment, person to person, at all levels of life and experience, symbolized by, expressed in and deepened through sexual union. This permanent personal and sexual partnership is publicly known, witnessed and accepted as such by society, and becomes within society the basis of a new family unit within which (normally and normatively) children are to be born and reared.

To make a fully valid marriage covenant would then involve mutual consent of the partners in commitment to such a relationship, and sexual union, together with some form of public witness and recognition. (Normally the commitment to marriage includes also the commitment to parenthood as part of its meaning. There are, however, certain circumstances in which this commitment to parenthood can be accepted as part of the normal meaning of marriage, although in this particular case it is impossible or unwise for it to be fulfilled.)

To this exposition of marriage as covenant, the following comments remain to be added.

(i) A further note on consent

Christian theology has insisted (on the above grounds) on the essential criterion of consent for valid marriage. By this is meant an understanding of and intention to fulfil the implications of a commitment to permanence, to exclusiveness, to love-faithfulness, to sexual union, to family. This requires the full and free consent of parties who are also legally and morally competent to give it. Duress or insanity in one or other partner or relationships of consanguinity or affinity between them, serve to nullify vows made by them. What is questionable, however, is the ground for nullity based on the concept of defective consent, taught for example by the Roman Catholic Church in some circumstances. While ignorance, and even psychological incapacity, may prove disastrous in the development of the sort of relationship described by 'one flesh', where there is evidence of a free and adequately informed consent given in the public exchange of solemn vow, and the relationship is sealed in sexual union, it appears clearer, and more biblical, to recognize that a marriage covenant has been made (albeit sometimes a 'bad' marriage), rather than affirm that, despite appearances, there never was a marriage at all. But this we will need to discuss more fully in a later chapter.

In his exposition of the Institution of Marriage, to which we have referred, O'Donovan makes the point that the couple in marriage submit to an order of necessity not of their own choosing. 'But', he goes on, 'we must qualify this immediately, and add that they marry only because they have freely chosen to. They do not have the choice *what*, but they do have the choice *whether*, and they do have the choice *whom*. This freedom, so much taken for granted by Western man, is a result of the impact of Christianity on the institution of marriage ... By insisting on "consent" as a criterion for a valid marriage, Christian theology has done much to weaken the practice of arranged marriages in societies where that practice once prevailed.'[51]

While it is unclear how strongly the consent of bride and groom featured in the making of marriage in Pentateuchal times, the gradual unfolding of the meaning of covenant made by vow of consent, paved the way for the Christian theology to which O'Donovan refers. The public vow of consent is thus the *terminus a quo* of the marriage covenant and it forms the basis for the recognition of marriage by society. Consent is the precondition of the establishment of the relationship described by 'one flesh'.[52]

Because the consent to marry includes the consent to a commitment to permanence, however, and is recognized as such by society, it does not follow that what is made by personal choice may be dissolved by personal choice alone. Divorce by mutual consent, based on a view of marriage as an arrangement terminable at will by the partners alone, finds no place in the understanding of marriage as covenant.

(ii) Divorce as 'covenant breaking'

If marriage is understood in covenant terms, then the possibility of divorce must be discussed as the possibility of breaking covenant. The covenant structure of marriage lends weight to the view, discussed earlier, that marriage is not a metaphysical status which cannot be destroyed; it is rather a moral commitment which should be honoured. The question of divorce should not therefore be framed as a question of metaphysical possibilities; it is to be asked rather within the area of moral law, and the moral permissibility of breaking covenant. Moreover, as we have said, there is more to covenant than simply terminable contract. A marriage covenant centering in the relationship of the partners is none the less more than that: it is a relationship within an external and socially recognized structure. The partners cannot therefore simply be free to dissolve their marriage at will: the covenant which they make on 'getting married' is a moral commitment to a permanent relationship and is known as such by others. The tragedy is that marriage relationships do in fact fail, and that society may agree that covenants are in fact broken. When they are, they signal a failure in keeping moral obligation; in these terms, to initiate divorce is not impossible, but sinful.

To understand divorce as a moral (rather than a metaphysical) question, however, allows us to consider whether and in what circumstances such a moral obligation as is undertaken in marriage may be overridden by other moral duties, and whether and in what circumstances, divorce may be considered the lesser evil. This will form the discussion of Chapter 5.

(iii) Covenant or sacrament?

It is arguable that what we called the 'absolute indissolubilist' tradition in the Church could never have arisen without the medieval conception of marriage as a sacrament. To be sure there is a 'sacramental theology of marriage' if by that is meant the theological need to root the meaning of marriage in God's creation and in the analogy between the marriage relationship and that between God and his people.[53] We have argued that the biblical description of marriage as covenant does justice to both these emphases.

The development of the sacramental analogy to affirm that marriage between baptized Christians is a full dominical sacrament of the Church in which husband and wife are joined by God in an unbreakable union, goes beyond Scriptural warrant, however. It leads, moreover, to what in our view is an erroneous way of framing the question of divorce. As we noted in our discussion of Augustine and of Luther, the fact that the Vulgate uses *sacramentum* to translate *musterion* in Eph. 5, gives no support to the view that marriage is one of the sacraments of the Church. The Report *Marriage and the Church's Task* was right therefore to reject the sacramental argument for indissolubility.[54] The covenant description safeguards all that is biblically warranted in the sacramental theology of marriage, but avoids the unbiblical metaphysical conclusions which that view implies.

(iv) Legal and ecclesiastical framework

If the essence of the divine institution of marriage is a bond of moral troth, then marriage should not be considered primarily as either a legal or an ecclesiastical institution. One of the problems of much Christian writing on marriage is that it has often understood marriage *only* in terms of its contractual or ecclesiastical external aspects. Much of what passes as a theology of marriage is in fact a 'theology' of the wedding ceremony. But the roles of the State and the Church are external to the covenant relationship itself. This is not of course to say that these external social aspects of marriage are unimportant. On the contrary, as we have argued, it is part of the nature of a covenant that it should be publicly acknowledged, and its responsibilities publicly accepted; it is part of Christian duty to act responsibly towards the society in which God calls one to live. Nevertheless the question 'Why should we "get married"?' (i.e. take part in a wedding ceremony) is more a question about Christian responsibility to society, than it is a question about the essential meaning of the marriage relationship. Theologically speaking, there is little difference between a church wedding ceremony and any other civil wedding ceremony, if the marriage covenant there promised and witnessed is the same. There is an obvious appropriateness in the setting of Christian worship for those who value the presence and prayer of Christian friends at their covenant-making. There is an obvious opportunity for Christian witness in the identification of the Christian Church with the ceremony by which two people commit themselves to each other in the God-ordained marriage ordinance. There is also an obvious pastoral opportunity for Christian teaching to be given to those who through tradition now seek out the Christian priest for their marriage, without necessarily professing the Christian faith. All this is gain, and the present wedding practice of the Church of England is valued for these reasons. But that is not to say that a wedding with the intention of making and maintaining covenant faithfulness in the sense in which we have expounded it, is any less a marriage, for lack of ecclesiastical context.

The questions on which the Christian Church needs to focus are not so much, therefore, questions of external and social discipline, as the 'internal' question: How best can the Church witness pastorally and institutionally to the Christian concept of the marriage covenant? How can the Church provide teaching, support and crisis-care in the understanding, strengthening and recovering of the meaning of covenant faithfulness? What sort of *commitment* is required for any particular wedding ceremony to be solemnized in church? To these questions we shall return.

We need first, however, to give space to the biblical and moral dimensions of the central questions concerning divorce.

SUMMARY OF CHAPTER 3

1 The primary biblical way of understanding marriage is in terms of covenant.

2 The interchange of analogies by which God's covenant with his people gives a meaning to human marriage, and vice versa, can be traced through both Old and New Testaments.

3 Five marks of comparison are given between divine covenant and human marriage: initiative of love; vow of consent; obligation of faithfulness; promise of blessing; centrality of sacrifice.

4 The human marriage covenant is made from the three strands: 'leaving father and mother', 'cleaving to the partner', becoming 'one flesh'. This is expounded in these terms:

    (i) 'one flesh' and the question of human sexuality;

    (ii) 'one flesh' and the foundation of the family;

    (iii) 'cleaving'; the central concept of covenant-fidelity;

    (iv) 'leaving', and the institutional framework for covenant relationship.

5 Consent is the *terminus a quo* of the covenant, and the precondition of the establishment of 'one flesh'.

6 If marriage is a covenant, then the possibility of divorce is the possibility of breaking covenant.

7 'Covenant' carries all that is biblically important in the broader Catholic (as distinct from Reformation and classical Anglican) notion of 'sacrament' as a sacred sign. 'Covenant' avoids the absoluteness of indissolubility which 'sacrament of marriage' has come to imply in many circles.

REFERENCES TO CHAPTER 3

1 K. Barth, *Church Dogmatics (CD)* (ET 1936 –), Vol. 3/4, for example.

2 e.g. Gen. 17:1ff; Exod. 2:24; 19:5ff; Ps. 89:20ff; Jer. 31:31; Ezek. 36:26ff; Mark 14:24; Heb. 10:12ff. G. J. Wenham describes the O.T. covenants as 'acts of divine grace – arrangements initiated by God out of his spontaneous mercy'. It seems likely that the Abrahamic-Davidic covenants are modelled on royal grants of land and dynasty, and that the Sinaitic covenant is modelled on a vassal treaty. In both cases man's obedient response to God is set in the context of his gracious promissory initiative. Cf. B. N. Kaye and G. J. Wenham (eds.), *Law, Morality and the Bible* (1978), p. 4f.

3 Ezek. 36:28; Heb. 8:10. Cf. also Lev. 11:44; Matt. 5:48; 1 Pet. 1:15f. with ref. to covenant terms; examples of covenant sign are rainbow (Gen. 9:12); circumcision (17:10); or baptism (cf. Col. 2: 11-12).

4 P. Ramsey, *Patient as Person* (1970), p. 4.

5 E. Schillebeeckx, *Marriage: Human Reality and Saving Mystery* (Sheed and Ward, 1965), pp. 32, 33.

6 It is interesting to note that even by Hosea's time the death penalty prescribed for adultery in the Mosaic legislation was not enforced, or not enforceable. Divorce was the appropriate response to adultery.

7 W. Shakespeare, *The Phoenix and the Turtle*.

8 Cf. *Book of Common Prayer*, 'The Form of Solemnization of Matrimony'.

9 Barth, *CD*, *3/1*, pp. 207-20.

10 Contrast, for example, G. C. Berkouwer, *Man: The Image of God* (Eerdmans, 1962), p. 72f.

11 R. J. Ehrlich, 'The Indissolubility of Marriage as a Theological Problem', *SJT*, *23/3* (1970), p. 298 (my parenthesis).

12 G. R. Dunstan, *Theology*, LXXVIII, No. 659 (May 1975), p. 245f.

13 This is true at least of marriage as we now know it in our culture. Dunstan notes that, of course, in other societies and at other times, the initiative may well have been from family to family, and not person to person. However, from the perspective of Eph. 5, for example, we agree with Dunstan that these are 'anticipations', and that given time and opportunity, the marriage union based on personal initiative of love does emerge. *Op. cit.*, p. 247.

14 *Ibid.*, p. 248.

15 *Ibid.*, p. 249.

16 *Ibid.*

17 We must be alert both to the danger of reading more into the narrative than it is intended to carry (cf. G. R. Dunstan's comments, *Theology*, May 1975, p. 245), and also to the important fact that, as we have seen, this passage is central in the Synoptic and Pauline exposition of a doctrine of marriage.

18 G. von Rad, *Genesis* (SCM, ET 1961), p. 82f.

19 Smedes, *Sex for Christians* (Eerdmans, 1977), p. 28.

20 Smedes, *op. cit.*, p. 29.

21 Barth, *op. cit.*

22 Smedes, *op. cit.*, p. 33.

23 As Paul Ramsey notes (*Nine Modern Moralists* (1962), p. 71f) in his essay on 'Sartre: Sex in Being' it is philosophers like Sartre in their emphasis on the passion of being for being in sexual encounter, who are nearer to the meaning of Gen. 2:24 than some theologians!

24 Smedes, *op. cit.*, p. 34.

25 H. Seebass in C. Brown (ed.), *The New International Dictionary of New Testament Theology* (Paternoster, 1975), p. 678.

26 G. R. Dunstan, *op. cit.*, p. 251.

27 D. S. Bailey, *The Mystery of Love and Marriage* (SCM, 1952), p. 44.

28 *Contra* e.g. J. D. M. Derrett, *Law in the New Testament* (Darton, Longman and Todd, 1970), p. 363f.

29 What Helen Oppenheimer calls 'the harvest of the Spirit', *The Marriage Bond* (Faith Press, 1976), p. 60f.

30 Cf. Gen. 29:14, 15; Jud. 9:2; 2 Sam. 5:1; 19:12-13. The *Hebrew and English Lexicon of the Old Testament* by F. Brown, S. R. Driver, C. A. Briggs, translates *basar* in 'one flesh' of Gen, 2:24 as 'one kindred, blood relation'. Cf. also Paul's reference to his kinsmen as 'my flesh' Rom. 9:3; 11:14.

31 Cf. here J. P. Sampley '*And The Two Shall Become One Flesh*'

(Cambridge, 1971), in which the author, by detailed analysis of traditions in the whole passage Eph. 5:21-33, affirms that the 'one flesh' clause quoted in v.31 can be understood not only of the uniting of two marriage partners, but also as 'the occasion for the introduction of organic terminology'. Since Gen. 2:24 states that 'the two shall become one flesh', it is possible for the author of Ephesians to speak of the man as head of the wife (v.23a) and Christ as head over the Church (v.23b). He interprets Gen. 2:24 to refer not only to human marriage, but also to the marriage of Christ and the Church. (*Op. cit.*, pp. 86ff, 147). Cf. also G. R. Dunstan, *Theology*, May 1975, p. 251.

32 Bailey, *op. cit.*, p. 50f.

33 Smedes, *op. cit.*, p. 129.

34 Bailey, *op. cit.*, p. 50f.

35 Smedes, *op. cit.*, p. 42ff.

36 U. Cassuto, *A Commentary on the Book of Genesis* Part 1, (The Magnes Press, Jerusalem, ET 1961), p. 137.

37 Cf. R. Fletcher, *The Family and Marriage in Britain* (Pelican, 1973)[3], p. 38.

38 Cf. von Rad, *op. cit.*, p. 82; and P. Ramsey, *One Flesh* (Grove, 1975).

39 Cf. C. C. Harris, *The Family*, Studies in Sociology (George Allen and Unwin, 1969), p. 87ff. Harris comments (p. 91), on suggestions and experiments to 'abolish the family' as a social unit: 'In order to explain the nature of the family we have had to argue that where, in consequence of the performance of activities of rearing, mates and children come to form a social group, this group persists even after its characteristic activities have ceased. It does not persist solely because the persons concerned are recognized as biologically related. If therefore we wanted to "farm" children, we should have to rear them in groups composed of them, a man and a woman. When the activities of rearing were over, we should expect to find that the grouping persisted. We should have therefore a social group made up of male and female rearers and their reared young. In other words we should have a group with the same sex generational structure as a family. It would be absurd, since the co-residence of the rearers is required, not to use persons having a sexual relationship with one another as the rearers. You would end up, therefore, with a family with only the biological links of parenthood missing.

'It would seem, therefore, very difficult to avoid having the family as a social institution, even if one wanted to.'

40 P. Ramsey, *One Flesh* (Grove, 1975).

41 Cf. also Gen. 34:3; Deut. 11:22; 13:4.

42 J. H. Olthuis, *I Pledge You My Troth* (Harper & Row, 1975), p. 21f.

43 Smedes, *op. cit.*, p. 167.

44 Here following the headings and exposition of Smedes, *op. cit.*, p. 167ff.

45 O. O'Donovan, *Marriage and Permanence* (Grove, 1978), p. 15.

46 Smedes, *op. cit.*, p. 180.

47 *Ibid.*, p. 181.

48 J. H. Olthuis art. 'Marriage' in C. F. H. Henry (ed.) *Baker's Dictionary of Christian Ethics* (Baker Book House, 1973), p. 408.

49 This is evident from the betrothal laws and other regulations of sexual behaviour in the Pentateuch (cf. esp. also Gen. 34:9; Deut. 7:3; Josh. 23:12) as well as the references to wedding festivities in the N.T. (Matt. 22:3; 22:8f; Lk. 12:36; 14:8; Jn. 2:1, 2; Rev. 19:7; 19:9) and to 'giving and being given in marriage' (Mk. 12:25; Matt. 22:30; 24:38; Lk. 17:27; 20:34; 1 Cor. 7:38).

50 O'Donovan, *op. cit.*, p. 4.

51 O'Donovan, *op. cit.*, p. 5f.

52 *Ibid.*

53 Cf. here H. Oppenheimer, *op. cit.*, p. 34f.

54 *Op. cit.* p. 49, para. 137.

CHAPTER 4

Divorce and Remarriage

*The Background and Exegesis of
the Biblical Material*

If, as we have argued the marriage covenant and sexual union belong together; and if the 'one flesh' union derives from the action of God in yoking husband and wife together in covenant partnership, the questions of divorce and of remarriage become: In what circumstances, if any, can the 'one flesh' union be severed, the marriage covenant be broken?; and if the marriage is broken, is a partner then set free to marry someone else? These are the questions to which the following chapters are addressed.

The biblical material on the question of divorce has, of course, been the subject of an extensive literature, and has been interpreted in many different ways. Indeed, one of the complications of the debates in the history of the Church on this question has been that all sides, Catholic, Protestant, and the various divisions of opinion within both, want to claim biblical backing for their case. Not only, moreover, is there a difference in understanding the meaning of the biblical texts, there is also the vexed question of their application into our cultural and ecclesiastical setting. We shall take up that second issue in subsequent discussion; the present chapter concentrates on a discussion of the biblical material in its own context.

This chapter falls into two main sections: 1. Old Testament Background, and 2. New Testament, the latter including: five introductory points; a discussion of the Synoptic divorce material ((a) Mk. 10:2-12; (b) Lk. 16:18; (c) Matt. 5:31-2 and

19:3ff, with an extended discussion of the *porneia* clauses; (d) remarriage after divorce); and finally the teaching of Paul in Romans 7 and 1 Corinthians 7.

The chapter concludes that in the Old Testament, in the Gospels and in the teaching of Paul, the law of God for the permanence of marriage is affirmed, but that also in each section of teaching, there is an indication of the need for specific legislation to regulate divorce in those circumstances in which, because of sin, God's intention is not maintained, or adhered to.

Old Testament Background

One of the most comprehensive recent accounts of the legal and social setting of the biblical material on marriage and divorce is given in an unpublished memorandum to the Church of Ireland Committee on the remarriage of divorced persons, by G. Wenham.[1] On the assumption that the people of ancient Israel shared the attitudes and customs of its contemporary neighbours unless there is explicit evidence to the contrary, Wenham comes to the following conclusions (we give a summary) about Old Testament marriage laws and customs:

First, the background to pre-exilic Old Testament laws is in many ways like that of eighteenth-century Mesopotamia (documented in the Laws of Hammurabi and the Laws of Eshunna), namely that marriage was commonly arranged by parents; financial considerations show that society intended marriage to be a lifelong commitment: betrothal was effected by handing over bride money to the bride's father (Gen. 24:53; 34:12; Deut. 22:29). Husbands expected fidelity from their wives, and could exact the death penalty for adultery (Deut. 22:22). It was quite possible for a man to divorce his wife, but unless the woman had put her husband to public shame, the cost was prohibitively high, and only the rich could have afforded it: the husband would have had to return the generous dowry to the wife's family. Wenham summarizes the situation: 'In today's terms, an adulterous woman could face the death penalty, and an adulterous man the loss of the whole of his estate.'[2] (i.e. in returned dowry.)

Secondly, post-exilic Old Testament literature reflects customs more similar to those of fifth-century Egypt (Elephantine). These are very like those of eighteenth-century Babylon except in three important respects: the price of divorce had fallen, and wages had risen; the women could sue for divorce as well as the men; the death penalty was not exacted for adultery.[3] In other words, in post-exilic times divorce was somewhat easier than earlier although, as Wenham comments, 'the laws were still drafted to make the marriage bond as durable as possible'.

An analysis of the Pentateuchal laws governing premarital intercourse, incest and adultery indicates that these laws were framed to preserve the view that in marriage a man and his wife are united together in what is intended to be expressed in a lifelong union.[4] Thus, if a man seduces a virgin who is not betrothed, and lies with her, then he must pay the bride money (50 shekels) to her father, and make her his wife; all subsequent right of divorce is lost. If the father utterly refuses to allow the marriage, he must still pay the bride money (Exod. 22:16-17; Deut. 22:28-9).

Sexual intercourse is forbidden between first and second degree relatives (Lev. 18:6-18), and the penalties for infringement are severe (Lev. 20:10–21). Part of the reason for the prohibition against 'uncovering the nakedness of your father's wife' is that 'it is your father's nakedness' (Lev. 18:8). In other words, 'father' and 'father's wife' are through marriage now in a close family relationship.

Adultery in the Pentateuchal laws is sexual intercourse between a married woman and a man who is not her husband.[5] Both adulterer or adulteress and their consorts were liable to the death penalty (Lev. 20:10; Deut. 22:22). The seventh commandment (Exod. 20:14) stands for the inviolability and permanence of marriage.[6] As Derrett points out, however,[7] the commandment reads 'Thou shalt not commit *na'af*. The Hebrew concept *na'af* is not identical with 'adultery' in the criminal sense just noted, nor with our modern technical sense. It rather refers, says Derrett, to the irregularity (and so impermissibility) of sexual relations outside the 'one flesh' union. The seventh commandment is not just against sexual sin: it is *for* the one flesh marriage covenant. (It is *na'af* that is translated by *moicheuo* in the Septuagint.)

The only Pentateuchal law directly relating to the practice of divorce is Deuteronomy 24:1-4. (This passage is the background to the New Testament discussion on divorce recorded in Mark 10:2ff and Matt. 19:3ff.)

> When a man takes a wife and marries her, if then she finds no favour in his eyes because he has found some indecency in her, and he writes her a bill of divorce and puts it in her hand and sends her out of his house, and she departs out of his house, and if she goes and becomes another man's wife, and the latter husband dislikes her and writes her a bill of divorce and puts it in her hand and sends her out of his house, or if the latter husband dies, who took her to be his wife, then her former husband, who sent her away, may not take her again to be his wife, after she has been defiled; for that is an abomination before the LORD, and you shall not bring guilt upon the land which the LORD your God gives you for an inheritance.

As most modern commentators agree, the protasis in this paragraph covers the first three verses, and it is only at the beginning of v.4 ('then her former husband . . .') that the apodosis is introduced.[8] This contrasts with older readings like the AV ('because he hath found some unseemly thing in her, that he shall write her a bill of divorce and give it into her hand, and send her out of his house') which could well be read as *requiring* the husband to divorce his wife should he find 'some unseemly thing' in her. The RSV agrees with modern commentators that the Deuteronomic legislation is a *permission* and not a *prescription*.[9] In other words, this passage does not make divorce mandatory; it does not even encourage or advise men to put away their wives if they are guilty of 'some indecency' (v.1). It cannot even be said to sanction divorce, though it recognizes that divorces happen (cf. Lev. 21:7, 14; 22:13; Num. 30:9) even though financial considerations, as we have seen, probably made them rare. This passage simply refuses the remarriage of a wife to her former husband after he has put her away and she has married someone else.[10] It also provides for a bill of divorcement to regulate the divorces which were tolerated, and it does appear that such a bill was mandatory.[11] This was probably to minimize the possibility of hasty divorce,[12] as well as to regulate the legal and social aspects of it.

What is the 'some indecency' for which the Mosaic legislation allows divorce to be legalized? This almost certainly did not mean adultery (which at that time was liable to the death penalty: Num. 20:10; Deut. 22:22f), nor suspected adultery (which was covered by Num. 5:11-31), nor premarital intercourse (which carried penalties from death, Deut. 22:20ff, to severe fine, Deut. 22:28). It meant rather some other (sexual?) misconduct which was sufficient to justify the withholding of heavy divorce duties which would be needed for a divorce if the wife were not guilty.[13] A. Isaksson,[14] noted that the expression occurs also in Deut. 23:14, and so suggests that in Deut. 24:1 it refers to the wife's indecent exposure. Calum M. Carmichael,[15] arguing from the formal arrangement of legal material in Deuteronomy, also thinks 'some indecency' refers to the embarrassment caused to the husband by the wife's public behaviour.[16]

Whatever the precise connotation of the phrase, Moses tolerated the husband's initiation of divorce proceedings, if the marriage had been broken in this way. It is important to note that Moses is talking about divorce (in the phrase 'bill of divorcement') and not just separation. Although Deut. 24:1 reads 'send her out of the house', the word 'divorce' in the 'bill of divorcement' (*kerithuth*) is related to the root (*karath*) meaning 'cut off', 'hew down'[17] and is used for hewing timber (1 Kings 5:18), amputation (Lev. 22:24) and decapitation (1 Sam. 17:51). It indicates the severing of what was once a living union.

After divorce, the right of the wife to marry again (though not to her first husband) is presupposed. Why (v.4) was she not to return to her first spouse? The text says that to do so is an 'abomination before the LORD'. Most commentators suggest that this is because the second marriage was considered to be adulterous and remarriage with the first husband would implicate him in condoning adultery. Wenham quotes Yaron's suggestion[18] that the point at issue was rather one of incest: the first marriage expresses the closest kinship between the man and his wife; divorce did not end this kinship, so if they want to marry again, it would be worse than marrying a brother or a sister (actions which are also said to 'bring guilt on the land' and 'be an abomination to the LORD', Lev. 18). It seems more plausible, however, to take this as a reference to the practice of loaning wives (which Derrett, quoting Breslawi[19] refers to as being a contemporary problem), which is here forbidden.

Whatever the specific cultic reason for this prohibition, however, several important moral principles are implicit:

In the first place, guarantees are provided against hasty or rash divorce,[20] a definite and substantial cause of marital breakdown must be evident, and Moses is effectively condemning divorces without adequate causes. Secondly, a proper legal procedure had to be used. This would both make public the termination of the first marriage, and so promote a sense of social responsibility, and also – and perhaps more importantly – give the divorced woman rights in law, by protecting her against the capital charge of adultery if she remarried. Thirdly, the specific prohibition against remarriage to the first husband is a restriction on the cruelty of husbands who might treat their wives as temporarily dispensable.

In other words, the Mosaic legislation affords a recognition of the fact of marriage breakdown, although divorce is not approved; it acknowledges the need for civil legislation for the sake of society and to secure protection to the divorced woman; it serves to legislate against cruelty.

When we turn on to consider post-exilic customs in Israel, we find possible hints that the practice of easier divorce in fifth-century Egypt[21] was paralleled in Israel. Thus Malachi needs to affirm God's will for marriage by reminding his hearers that 'God hates divorce' (Mal. 2:16).[22] Despite the Deuteronomic permission, divorce is never God's will.

A different situation is described in Ezra 10 (cf. also Neh. 13:23ff). Ezra agrees that Israelites who had married foreign women should put away their wives. He was insisting that marriages with 'foreign women' (v.2 cf. 9:1f) were contrary to the law (cf. Deut. 7:3; Exod. 34:16) and should be declared null. Now sexual intercourse, albeit unlawfully, had taken place (v.3), yet the marriages were nullified. It is of interest to note that what theologically was regarded as a nullity was handled socially as a divorce.

Throughout the Old Testament, whenever divorce occurred the right of remarriage was presupposed. Rather than argue, as Derrett does, for example[23] that when a divorce proceeded according to the Mosaic legislation, the first union in God's sight was still in existence despite the legal divorce, and in any subsequent union sexual intercourse should be prohibited, the natural reading of Deut. 24:1ff. would indicate that when a man put away his wife, the couple's marriage ceased (even though a certain family relationship remained), and they were free to remarry (though not each other). This is certainly the way in which the Mishnah interpreted the situation. 'The essential formula in the bill of divorce is "Lo, thou art free to marry any man".' R. Judah says: ' "Let this be from me thy writ of divorce and letter of dismissal and deed of liberation, that thou mayest marry what soever man thou wilt." The essential formula in a writ of emancipation is "Lo thou are a freedwoman; lo, thou belongest to thyself".'[24]

To summarize, therefore: the Old Testament marriage laws, often with corresponding heavy penalties associated, were framed to preserve the view that God's intention for marriage was of a lifelong permanent union. However, because of what Jesus later described as the 'hardness of men's hearts' (cf.

Matt. 19:8) there were circumstances in which the severing of the marriage bond was tolerated. There is no sense, however, that divorce is mandatory on the husband, even if his wife is guilty of 'some indecency'. Divorce is never encouraged or commanded. Rather the restriction imposed (no remarriage to the first husband) and the reason given (an 'abomination before the LORD') was intended as strong discouragement of easy divorce. Indeed, taking the divine relationship with Israel as a pattern, there was – certainly in Hosea's day and Isaiah's day for example, – an encouragement to seek forgiveness and reconciliation (Hos. 3:1ff; Isa. 50:1ff, etc.).

New Testament

The New Testament divorce material was written in a context in which it is largely true both that the Old Testament law was held dear (although it was variously interpreted), and also that Greek and Roman customs were exercising some influence.[25] The following introductory points need to be isolated.

(a) First, there was in Jesus' day a dispute growing between the Pharisaic schools about what constituted proper grounds for divorce. The Hillelite school interpreted the Deuteronomic legislation very freely; the Shammaites were much more strict. The Mishnah records the dispute:

> The School of Shammai say: A man may not divorce his wife unless he has found unchastity in her, for it is written, *Because he hath found in her* indecency *in anything*. And the school of Hillel say: (He may divorce her) even if she spoiled a dish for him, for it is written: *Because he hath found in her indecency in* anything. R. Akiba says: Even if he found another fairer than she, for it is written: *And it shall be if she find no* favour in his eyes . . .[26]

In Jesus' day, the question of 'grounds for divorce' was an issue turning on the interpretation of Deut. 24:1ff, and this dispute lies behind the way Matthew records the Pharisees' question to Jesus in Matt. 19:3: 'Is it lawful to divorce one's wife *for any cause*?' (contrast Mark 10:2). Prior to AD 70 there was a period when the Shammaites could regularly out-vote the Hillelites, and certainly the former were very influential at the time of Jesus (to judge by the disputes between them and Jesus on the matter of the Sabbath – over which the Hillelites would have had little cause for disagreement with Jesus). However, despite their stricter teaching on the question of divorce, allowing divorce only on grounds of the wife's unchastity, it is less certain that the actual practice of the Shammaites was any more strict than that of the school of Hillel. The Hellenist writer Philo implies that there was a whole variety of accepted grounds for divorce at the time of Christ, and he speaks of divorce as the woman's 'misfortune', not something that she has brought upon herself.[27] Writing half a century later, Josephus, himself a Pharisee,[28] who to judge from his share in the Jewish revolt may well have had Shammaite sympathies, tells us that he had three wives in all, the second of whom he 'divorced . . . as not pleased with her behaviour', and married a third time.[29] He also teaches that if a man desires to be divorced from his wife 'for any cause whatsoever (and many such causes happen among men)', he should give her in writing an assurance that he will not 'use her as his wife' any more; by this means she is set at liberty to marry another husband after receiving such a divorce bill, but if she is misused by the second husband she is not allowed to return to the first.[30]

After AD 70 for certain, and probably before, the laxer Hillelite school came to prevail. The Mishnah refers to the practice by which husbands were allowed to put away their wives even without payment of the *ketubah* (divorce money) if she 'transgresses the law of Moses' (by giving her husband untithed food, Num. 18:21; by 'having connexion with him in her uncleanness', Lev. 18:19; by not setting apart the Dough offering, Num. 15:18; or by not fulfilling a vow she has uttered, Deut. 23:21) or if she 'transgresses Jewish custom' (by going out with her hair unbound, by spinning in the street or speaking with any man, by cursing her husband's parents in his presence, or by being a 'scolding woman', defined as speaking inside her house so that the neighbours could hear her voice).[31]

Probably, therefore, we are right in inferring that divorce on fairly trivial grounds was relatively common in the time of Christ, and that even the stricter Shammaites did not practise what they preached (cf. Matt. 23:4).

(b) The second introductory point is that marriage and divorce were apparently cheaper, and therefore probably more common on that score also, than in earlier times.[32]

(c) Thirdly, despite the relative ease of divorce, godly Jews still maintained a very high view of marriage which considered the possibility of divorce only in terms of domestic tragedy for which 'the very altar of God sheds tears', and for that reason believed that 'he who dismisseth his wife is hated by God'.[33] Yet, with all their abhorrence of divorce, as Rabbi Epstein noted, the Sages held 'the continuance of intimate relations between husband and wife after the bonds of affection were snapped to be immoral, and the offspring of such a union was regarded by them as morally unhealthy, belonging to the class of "rebels" and such as "transgress against God" '.[34] The result of this attitude was twofold. The rabbis instituted a number of measures (like the *ketubah* payment referred to) to check against the abuse of divorce law. But they also 'refused to blind themselves to the harsh realities of life when divorce with the freedom to remarry could come as the only release from a galling relationship which discordant natures and unequal tempers had rendered intolerable' (Epstein).[35]

(d) Fourthly, it seems extremely unlikely that in the time of Christ, the Jewish courts were allowed to carry out the death penalty for adultery.[36] Indeed, even in Hosea's day (eighth century), the exaction of the death penalty for adultery does not seem to have been operative, and in the New Testament it is assumed that divorce is the only penalty. John 8:5 quotes the letter of the Deuteronomic law, but the way this test case was set up implies that the penalty was not enforced or not enforceable (indeed, it may have been to pose Jesus with a choice between the current civil law and the letter of the torah). L. M. Epstein says that capital punishment for adultery was meant by the rabbis to remain a theoretical teaching, but was not favoured as a practical penal guide for the courts.[37]

Certainly by the time of the Mishnah, divorce was the required penalty for proven adultery, and when adultery was detected, the adulterous woman was forbidden by the court both to her husband and to her paramour.[38] Israelite courts could indeed *compel* a Jewish husband to divorce his wife on accepted grounds.[39] It is certain therefore that Jesus' hearers would have assumed that the law of divorce was relevant to the crime of adultery, and highly probable that they would have assumed that divorce after adultery was mandatory.

(e) Fifthly, in the Gentile world, women could initiate divorce proceedings against their husbands, as well as husbands against their wives, which probably accounts for the peculiarly Markan reference to that practice in Mark 10:12. Josephus refers to the possibility of a Jewish wife initiating proceedings against her husband, but he says that it is not a Jewish custom.[40] What was allowed to Jewish women, however, was a wife's freedom to petition the court to require her husband to divorce her in certain circumstances (such as if the husband had certain diseases or engaged in certain occupations).[41] A woman might even write her own divorce bill for her husband to sign,[42] or 'compel him until he says "It is my will" '.[43]

In the Gentile world, however, no document was legally necessary, and since Roman marriage, for instance, depended merely on intention it could be brought to an end by the free will of either or both parties.[44] In 19-18 BC Augustus did require in some cases a declaration of divorce before seven witnesses, and made adultery a crime for which divorce was mandatory. (If adultery was proved, the wife and her paramour were banished to different islands.[45]) If a husband failed to divorce his wife for adultery under the Augustan law, he himself could face prosecution for condonement.[46] We can properly assume, therefore, that Gentile readers under Roman law would, like Jews, have taken it for granted that divorce following adultery was legally required.

The Synoptic Material
(*Matt. 5:31f; Matt. 19:3ff; Mark 10:2ff; Luke 16:18*)

It is not helpful to our main task to give a detailed discussion of the Synoptic problems posed by the divorce material.[47] Our aim is to draw out the main themes of the teaching of Jesus as it is presented by the evangelists, and to discuss such differences as affect our understanding of these main themes.

The most extensive discussions are found in Matt. 19 and Mark 10, in which Jesus is being 'tested' on the question of divorce. We note briefly the divergences between the two accounts. For Matthew, the questioners are Pharisees; they are unnamed in some of the texts of Mark 10:2. For Matthew (19:3) the question posed to 'test' Jesus was that concerning the grounds for divorce ('for any cause?'); for Mark (10:2), the test point was about the legitimacy of divorce at all. The dialogue then follows a different order. In Mark, Jesus speaks of the Mosaic permission (10:4) as a 'commandment' (10:5) (though it is legitimate to interpret this 'commandment' as a reference to the mandatory requirement of the divorce certificate, and not a commandment to divorce as such); he then refers to Gen. 1:27 and 2:24. In Matthew's account, the Genesis quotations come first, and Jesus speaks then of Moses' word (about divorce) as a 'concession' (19:8). Matthew omits the reference in Mark 10:12 to the woman's initiative in taking out divorce proceedings, presumably because this had no relevance to his Jewish readership. Matthew alone adds the discussion concerning eunuchs (Matt. 19:10-12), unparalleled elsewhere in the Gospels. Most significant of all for our purpose, Matthew adds an exceptive clause (19:9; cf. 5:32) to the saying about divorce, the meaning of which we shall need to discuss in some detail later.

Most commentators regard these divergences of detail as evidence for the priority of Mark, and see the alterations as evidence of Matthew's editorial activity.[48] Others[49] have affirmed the more primitive nature of Matthew's account (the way the Pharisees' question is posed, for example), or argued for the literary independence of the two traditions.

Despite divergences of detail, however, the main thrust of both passages is identical. Both evangelists teach that Jesus responds to the question of divorce by first affirming God's will for marriage. He refers to Gen. 1:27 and 2:24, using the latter to expound the former: marriage is the permanent exclusive 'one flesh' bond created by the linking together of a man and a woman by God.

Jesus then gives his climactic unconditional statement on marriage: 'What therefore God has joined together, let no man put asunder.' (Matt. 19:6; Mark 10:9). This is a reference both to the fact that marriage is a divine institution,[50] and also to the fact that any initiative taken to 'put asunder' the bond of marriage is contrary to God's will. The phrase 'let not . . .' is a moral commandment; it does not express an impossibility.

It is in the light of this unconditional affirmation of God's intention for marriage, that we must examine the statements about divorce.

(a) Mark 10:2-12

We begin with Mark 10:2ff, in which Jesus distinguishes between the Deuteronomic legislation (expounded as a sign of Israel's 'hardness of heart' and their failure to believe and obey God)[51] on the one hand, and God's will for marriage on the other. *Sklerokardia* carries the sense of wilful obstinacy against the will of God (cf. the *LXX* of Deut. 10:16; Jer. 4:4, for example).

Many commentators take this contrast an an abrogation by Jesus of the Deuteronomic legislation, and a sharp antithesis between Moses and Jesus on the questions of divorce.[52] However, there is no specific rejection of the Mosaic provision. Indeed in v.5 the requirement of a certificate is described as a 'commandment' – of God through Moses – for a specific purpose. We shall argue in the next chapter that it is illegitimate to pose an antithesis between Jesus and Moses. The contrast is rather between what we may call a 'creation principle' and the need – in Moses' day – for civil regulation within a sinful world. Whether the coming of Jesus has changed the need for such a regulation is a matter for discussion (see next chapter); we do not think it has.[53]

Having affirmed God's will for marriage, and the prohibition against initiating divorce (Mark 10:9), Jesus then (vv. 11-12) privately to the disciples expands his meaning by speaking of divorce and remarriage as 'adultery'.

> Whoever divorces his wife and marries another, commits adultery against her; and if she divorces her husband and marries another, she commits adultery.[54]

We must first comment on the meaning of *apoluein*, translated 'divorce'. The Arndt-Gingrich Lexicon defines it to mean 'let go, send away, dismiss' in this context, and the older versions are right therefore to give the sense of 'put away' one's spouse. We are not concerned here primarily with the legal form of divorce procedure, but with the personal initiative which breaks the marriage union. There are those who believe that because *apoluo* occurs on the lips of Jesus only in the context of divorce *and remarry*, he can only mean 'separate' and not divorce in the sense of dissolving the bond of marriage. This view is taken by most Roman Catholic commentators.[55] It seems the more natural sense of the passage here, however, to affirm that Jesus is speaking of divorce as severance of the marriage bond, partly because the whole discussion is set in the context of Deuteronomy 24 which concerns divorce, partly because the idea of separation from bed and board was a concept not common to the Jews (although arguably Jesus could have initiated it: it is unlikely that without further explanation, his hearers would have understood him, however), and partly because it is likely that in Jesus' day divorce was practically automatically followed by remarriage (which arguably Jesus could be forbidding, though again in the context of a discussion of Deut. 24 – which assumes remarriage – it is unlikely that this would have been understood from what Jesus is recorded to have said).

If right of remarriage after divorce was assumed, however, then divorce-and-remarriage belong together in Jesus' thinking, and we may understand the central thrust of his condemnation to be focused on the wrong of 'putting away', rather than on the remarriage which in this *ad hominem* discussion is the inevitable consequence. The guilt for the 'adultery' in the remarriage (10:11) lies with the one who has taken the initiative in 'putting away'. This is more explicit in Matt. 5:32, where the reading is 'Every one who divorces his wife . . . makes her an adulteress' (by forcing her to remarry or become a prostitute? We omit the 'exceptive clause' which will be considered later).

In other words, it is the act of divorce, the initiative in 'putting away', which brings Jesus' condemnation.

(b) Luke 16:18

Jesus' teaching in Mark 10:11 is paralleled in Luke 16:18, with one significant addition. Whereas Mark goes on (v. 12) to speak of the woman's initiative in divorce, Luke adds: 'He who marries a woman divorced from her husband commits adultery.'

Here again, Jesus is speaking of 'divorce-and-remarriage' under the sin of adultery. Commentators are divided on the implications of the second clause. It is possible that Jesus had in mind the particular situation of Herod and Herodias.[56] It is possible that in referring to 'he who marries a woman divorced from her husband' Jesus is thinking of the 'third party' in divorce proceedings: the woman is divorced in order to marry this other man, who is thereby implicated in the sin of the divorce. It may mean that there are lasting covenant obligations on the partners to the first marriage despite the legal divorce which, though the relationship is severed, the divorce does not remove. The second marriage then falls under the shadow of the broken covenant of the first, and both partners in the second marriage are party to a situation in which God's will for marriage in the 'one flesh' has been sinned against. Perhaps most likely, here as elsewhere, Jesus is criticizing the inequalities of a male-dominated society in which wives could be lightly divorced. One who treated his wife lightly in this way was committing adultery against her, and also encouraging some third party to commit adultery against him.[57]

Whichever alternative we choose, it is less likely to be the remarriage which is condemned, as the wrongful dismissal by the first husband.

(c) Matt 5:31-2 and Matt. 19:3ff

The first of the Matthean passages parallels Luke 16:18 and Mark 10:11-12, and the longer section in Matthew 19 parallels Mark 10:2-9.

As we have seen, the emphasis in Matt. 5:32 is on the responsibility of the husband not to divorce his wife, and *his* guilt if he does so (v. 32). It is noteworthy that, as we shall discuss in more detail in the next chapter, this section of the Sermon on the Mount is part of an exposition of the seventh commandment, referred to in Matt. 5:27. Just as Matt. 5:34-7 are concerned in part with the meaning of the eighth (Matt. 5:33a), so the condemnation of lustful looks (5:28ff) and of divorce (32) come as part of the exposition of the intention of the seventh commandment. (v. 31. 'It was also said . . .' introduces a subsection of the paragraph beginning in v. 27.[58]) We are therefore to conclude that Jesus is bringing the question of divorce within the meaning of 'Thou shalt not commit adultery'. As we have said, this commandment was directed at the preservation of 'one flesh' marriage; divorce, then, in the mind of

Jesus is tantamount to adultery, in that the 'one flesh' is broken.

Jesus is here expounding the 'inner' meaning of 'adultery', widening it to include any unfaithfulness (of thoughts 5:28, or actions) in territory which is intended to be kept only for the relationship described by 'one flesh'. Just as covenant-breaking in, for example, Ezekiel 16, is described in terms of 'adultery', so here in Matt. 5, Jesus is including the breaking of the marriage covenant in divorce within the meaning of 'Thou shalt not commit adultery'. It is arguable, though perhaps less likely, that *moicheuo* (which translates the *na'af* of the seventh commandment) in Mark 10:11-12 could refer to the sin of covenant-unfaithfulness generally. The same root occurs in Jas. 4:4 to describe 'unfaithful creatures' who break faith with God; it is used of the unfaithfulness of Israel, 'an evil and adulterous generation' (Matt. 12:39; 16:4); it describes the unfaithfulness of those 'who tolerate the woman Jezebel' in Rev. 2:22. Does Mark 10:11 then mean 'Every one who divorces his wife (and marries another) is guilty of the sin of covenant-unfaithfulness'?

Certainly, from Matt. 5:27-32, we learn that 'adultery' includes all the ways in which unfaithfulness in the marriage relationship can occur.

There is a significant addition in Matt. 5:32 – the 'exceptive clause' *parektos logou porneias*. This clause and its parallel in Matt. 19:9 (*me epi porneia*), have formed the basis in Protestant tradition for the view that adultery can be grounds for dissolution of the marriage bond. That this clause is a crux of interpretation is well known, and there are several surveys of the main possibilities of its meaning.[59]

We give a brief summary of the options (based on the assumption that the clause is authentic to the Matthean text).[60] We need, in judging between them, to attempt to account for the fact that it occurs in contexts in which Jesus is referring to the Deuteronomic legislation; to account for its presence in Matthew, but its absence in Mark and Luke, and the lack of any reference in the Epistles; we need also to bear in mind the

eventual quieting of the Pharisees, and also the reaction of
dismay from the disciples ('if such is the case of a man with his
wife, it is not expedient to marry', Matt. 19:10).

C. R. Fielding[61] believes that, in Matt. 5:32 in particular,
more has been read into the clause than the text demands. He
takes it to be simply Matthew's rather particular way of giving
detail, in this case pointing out a matter of fact (and not
changing the sense of the verse at all). If the wife has already
committed adultery (so Fielding reads '*porneia*'), then her
husband cannot be held guilty of *making* her an adulteress (5:32)
by divorcing her.

On this view, the appearance of an exceptive clause again in
19:9 is explained as a piece of Matthean editorial activity:

> In opposition to the Pharisees of his own day, Matthew attempted
> to bring together the attack on divorce which he found in Mark
> and the perfectly compatible doctrine of 5:32, and in doing so
> produced the awkward construction represented by 19:9.[62]

The overwhelming difficulty in taking *porneia* and *moicheia* as
synonymns, however, is that elsewhere in Matthew (15:19; cf.
also Mark 7:22; 1 Cor. 6:9; Heb. 14:4), *porneia* and 'adultery'
are referred to together, and carefully distinguished. If *porneia*
is not synonymous with *moicheuo*, however, what does it mean?

The view has been argued that *porneia* refers to betrothal, or
intercourse, within the prohibited degrees of Lev. 18:7-18.
Porneia can mean this, it is true (and probably has this reference
in Acts 15:20, 29 and in 1 Cor. 5:1)[63] but to restrict its use in
this way in the Matthean divorce passages is to go against the
order of the argument which has been about marriage and
divorce, and not about invalid unions. 'The reader can be
expected to understand it in this specialized sense only if there
is some indication in the context.'[64] As Vawter comments: 'Why
should Christ have introduced gratuitously a matter governed
by entirely different legislation, concerning which there was no
controversy, and about which the Pharisees needed neither re-
assuring nor correction?'[65]

Precisely the same point counts against the suggestion by Isaksson and others[66] that *porneia* refers only to premarital unchastity by the woman during the period of betrothal. This again was governed by separate legislation (Deut. 22). Indeed, Malina[67] argues that aside from one (debatable) instance there is no evidence that in traditional or contemporary usage the word *porneia* was taken to mean 'pre-betrothal, premarital, heterosexual intercourse of a non-cultic or non-commercial nature – i.e. what we call fornication today'. Malina's case has been strongly criticized, however, by J. Jensen[68] and others. Jensen believes that there is no basis for denying that the New Testament could use *porneia* to designate simple fornication, for the term demonstrably has a wide range of meanings. He concludes that it means sexual immorality in a fairly general sense, and does certainly include 'fornication' in our modern sense.

A. Mahoney[69] suggests that *porneia* means 'something offensive to the eyes of God', and believes that Jesus is saying that the 'unseemly thing' of Deut. 24:1 has a significance Godward. The implication in the Matthean passages would then be that mixed marriages in which one spouse is not a Christian are not under the general rule of indissolubility. This unusual suggestion seems unlikely in the context of the Pharisees' dispute. There is no other Gospel parallel, and no word from Jesus concerning mixed marriages had reached Paul by the time he wrote 1 Cor. 7:12.

It seems more satisfactory to regard the reference to *porneia* in the Matthean contexts as a specific reference back to the 'some indecency' of Deut. 24:1. This is supported by the parallel between *'erwat dabar* ('something unseemly') in Deut. 24:1 and *d^ebar 'erwat* ('a matter of unchastity'), as Hill translates it.[70] *Porneia* on the lips of Jesus would then be an exposition of the 'some indecency' of Deut. 24:1. It is not necessary to regard this as a direct translation, however. Indeed, it is much more likely to be an updating of the significance of the Mosaic expression into the cultural situation in which Jesus was speaking, in which, for example, the penalty for adultery was no longer death but divorce. To judge from the recent scholarly views of contemporary usage, *porneia* has a fairly wide reference,[71] and on the lips of Jesus means unlawful sexual conduct. Such conduct would include adultery, and without doubt, *porneia* included *moicheia* within its meaning, as its usage in the Septuagint demonstrates.[72]

We can conclude, therefore, that *porneia* in contemporary usage includes every kind of unlawful extramarital sexual misbehaviour, where in this context 'unlawful' means 'forbidden by the torah' (viz. cultic or commercial prostitution, 'indecency', fornication, incest, adultery).

What, then, can the 'exceptive clauses' mean in their Matthean context?[73] What function is *porneia* serving in these passages? Traditionally Protestant theologians have read *parektos logou porneias* (5:32) and *me epi porneia* (19:9), as exceptions to the general condemnation of 'divorce and remarriage' as adultery. Thus an exception is made 'on grounds of *porneia*' to the rule that a man makes his wife an adulteress if he divorces her (5:32), and to the rule that whoever divorces his wife and marries another commits adultery (19:9). Taking *porneia* to mean 'unlawful sexual conduct, including adultery, forbidden by the torah', Jesus, on this view, appears to be regarding such behaviour as 'grounds for divorce'. However, we recall that in certain specified circumstances the Jewish husband was compelled by civil law to divorce his wife, and this reference by Jesus need be understood as no more than an acknowledgement of the fact that a man does not sin by obeying that civil law. Certainly where the marriage has broken down because of *porneia* on the part of one partner, the other does not bear the guilt of the breakdown, even though he may be required to take the initiative in legal proceedings. The clause can hardly be used as the one prescriptive 'ground for divorce' of which Jesus can be said to approve.

The exceptive clauses in Matt. 5, 19, rather function as references to the need in a sinful society for civil legislation to regulate divorce. Jesus is drawing a distinction between the ideal (Gen. 2:24) and the actual – in which civil legislation is a 'permission' (Matt. 19:8) necessary because of 'hardness of heart'. (A contrast paralleled by Paul in 1 Cor. 7 – see below.) The precise way in which the civil Jewish legislation worked in Jesus' day was determined by torah.

To read the *porneia* clauses in this 'exceptive' way is linguistically valid. It fits the context of a discussion of Deuteronomy 24, and updates that legislation into the contemporary situation. It does, though, seem to align Jesus with the Shammaite school of thought, which in the light of his teaching that a righteousness is needed which 'exceeds that of the scribes and Pharisees' (Matt. 5:20) may be rather surprising. Further, the dismayed reaction of the disciples in Matt. 19:10 is on the face of it also surprising if on the matter of divorce, all one needed to do was be a Shammaite. This is not such a great objection as it appears, however, when it is remembered that the Shammaites' practice may well not have been as scrupulous as their teaching on this matter and in any case Jesus' primary point was an affirmation of the permanent nature of marriage in God's will, not the legalistic question as to what counted as proper grounds for divorce, which appears to have been the preoccupation of Shammaites and Hillelites alike.

In any case, Jesus' disagreement with the Pharisees is not so much in their understanding of Deut. 24, but in their application of it which ignored the fundamental doctrines of Gen. 1 and 2.

We would then account for the discrepancy between Matthew and Mark not in terms of modification or addition, but from the fact that Matthew's regard for his Jewish readership has a particular concern for questions of law and order. Mark and Luke in their blanket condemnation of divorce-and-remarriage as 'adultery' are giving the general rule which Jesus affirms as God's will for marriage. They are not referring to the circumstances in which the civil law compelled divorce (as it did in both Jewish and Roman contemporary law), which could quite properly be assumed. Matthew makes the assumption explicit, and gives the general rule in absolute terms, along with the exception necessary within a sinful society.

There is another way of approaching the *porneia* clauses, however, which deserves careful consideration.[74] Vawter calls this a 'preteritive' interpretation, which he traces back to Augustine (although Augustine used it for a different purpose). On this view the *porneia* clauses are preteritions, that is, they are not simply exceptions to the verbs 'put away and remarry' but are parenthetical comments on the whole statement. Vawter says that *me* in 19:9 should be understood simply as a negative particle nullifying *epi*, the latter signifying a circumstance or state, so that the phrase *me epi porneia* should be read '*porneia* is not involved'. (Banks parallels this with *me en te eorte* in Matt. 26:5 considered in relation to the whole of the preceeding verse[75]). In Matt. 5:32, *parektos* is read in an 'exclusive' sense, but with the wider meaning of 'outside, without, apart from', and the phrase then has the meaning 'quite apart from the matter of *porneia*'.

On this construction, and taking *porneia* itself as we did earlier as a reference back to the 'some indecency' of Deut. 24:1, the *porneia* sayings may then be generally translated:

> I say to you, whoever dismisses his wife – the permission of Deut. 24:1 notwithstanding – and marries another, commits adultery.

This has the advantage, particularly 'n 5:32, of linguistic simplicity. It also brings the main thrust of the Matthean passage exactly into line with Mark and Luke. It also does justice to the context of the discussion with the Pharisees concerning the exegesis of Deut. 24:1. Whether this is taken as the *ipsissima verba* of Jesus, or as most scholars tend to assume, a Matthean addition (which none the less we affirm to be an application of the mind of Jesus), the *porneia* clause in 19:9 fits well as a parenthesis qualifying the whole statement of Jesus in the dispute with the Pharisees, and not as a single exception to the otherwise absolute condemnation of divorce. (If it is indeed a Matthean addition, this would be in line with Matthew's other explanatory additions, such as Matt. 15:20b, and not a contradictory amendment of Jesus' intention, as some scholars have argued.) Against this view, however, it may be urged that the primary point of Jesus' reply is the contrast between the ideal and the actual (the 'Moses of Genesis' and the 'Moses of Deuteronomy') – a contrast that is lost in Vawter's construction.

Whichever way we decide on the *porneia* clauses, taking them as preteritions, or exceptions, the primary emphasis of Jesus' teaching is unmistakable: in the will of God for marriage, divorce has no place, and to initiate the 'putting away' of one's spouse infringes the seventh commandment. This strong view, which cut against both Hillelite and Shammaite acceptance of the legitimacy and indeed normality of divorce in certain circumstances, is quite sufficient to account for the surprised reaction of the disciples in 19:10: 'If such is the case of a man with his wife, it is not expedient to marry.' Jesus, however, implies that marriage is still to be the norm, in his teaching that the call to celibacy is a special calling (for those who through physical incapacity or a deliberate decision to refrain from marriage for the sake of the kingdom of heaven, live without normal marriage relations, 19:12). This is not expected of all (v. 11).[76]

(d) Remarriage after divorce

The assumption that remarriage normally follows divorce underlies all the Synoptic references to divorce. It was certainly assumed in the Deuteronomic legislation which forms the background to Matt. 19 and Mark 10. It was taken for granted in rabbinic Judaism,[77] and – taking *apoluo* on the lips of Jesus to mean divorce and not simply separation from bed and board, as we have argued – is taken for granted in Jesus' statements also.[78]

It is divorce, not remarriage, which is the centre of Jesus' condemnation; the sin is the 'adulterous' sin of covenant-breaking described in the Gospels as 'putting away' the spouse.

Having said that, however, in that remarriage is equated with adultery (Mark 10:11; Luke 16:18), even though the guilt for it rests on the one who takes the initiative in 'putting away' (Matt. 5:32), remarriage falls under the cloud of the broken covenant of the first marriage. Indeed, it is arguable that certain covenant obligations remain on the divorced partners, even though the marriage relationship has ceased.

Paul

The apostle Paul reaffirms the teaching of Christ in stressing the permanence of marriage. In Romans 7:2-3 he writes:

> A married woman is bound by law to her husband as long as he lives; but if her husband dies she is discharged from the law concerning the husband. Accordingly, she will be called an adulteress if she lives with another man while her husband is alive. But if her husband dies she is free from that law, and if she marries another man she is not an adulteress.

This passage serves as an illustration for Paul of the point he is making in 7:1, that 'the law is binding on a person only during his life'. It is to be presumed (by comparison with 3:19; 5:13; 1 Cor. 9:8, 9; 14:21; Gal. 3:10, 19) that 'the law' here refers to the Old Testament law, specifically that of Moses (although arguably it could be Roman law). In other words, v. 1 states the general principle that the law is binding for life; when the man dies, the dominion of law is dissolved. The law for marriage is used as an illustration of this general principle (vv. 2-3). While, therefore, it affirms that God's will for marriage is for life, and that if while her husband lives, a wife is married to another she commits adultery, it does not thereby make any judgement on the *possibility* of divorce – but only on its wrongness. Further, whether Paul is referring to Mosaic or Roman law, his readers in either case knew that by their law, divorce was tolerated in certain circumstances, and marriages could be dissolved even during the lifetime of the husband. The fact that he does not say so in this passage, which is primarily an illustration of a different point, indicates that Paul thought such an exception could properly be assumed without comment.

This may parallel the similar omissions in Mark and Luke.

1 Cor. 7

Verses 7-10 of 1 Cor. 7 summarize what Paul believed Jesus taught concerning marriage for Christian believers. The wife should not separate from her husband, and the husband should not divorce his wife. In other words, no initiative to break the marriage (putting away the wife by the husband, or wilful desertion by the wife) is to be taken. Paul does in parenthesis, however, recognize that this rule is not always obeyed. If a wife *does* separate from her husband, she should remain single or else be reconciled. This is not to be understood as teaching that Paul condemns divorce but allows separation. Rather, as Catchpole[79] comments, v. 11a, sandwiched between 10b and 11b which affirm the principle of the permanence of marriage, 'is to be taken as a situational parenthesis in which a less than ideal situation has posed a problem and receives solution'. Indeed the very purpose of remaining single, or else being reconciled, may presuppose a situation in which the husband is willing for reconciliation. Paul does not give a ruling for the case in which that supposition is false; is a wife who, for safety's sake, has been forced to flee from a cruel husband, but with no desire of her own to break up the marriage, consigned to celibacy for life?

Likewise, Paul's ruling against the husband taking the initiative in divorce is a word against wrongful dismissal by the husband. Paul does not treat the situation in which the husband would by law be required to divorce his wife because of her covenant-breaking behaviour against him.

By his parenthetical comment in v. 11a, however, Paul shows his willingness to apply the absolute will of Christ concerning marriage to the specific (and complex) needs of the Corinthian situation. He therefore has to make distinctions in his 'case law' which are not apparent in the Synoptic accounts of the words of Jesus.[80]

The same procedure is evident in vv. 12-16 in which Paul

takes up another problem in the Corinthian situation in which he specifically says he has no word from the Lord, namely the behaviour to be required of a Christian partner when an unbelieving partner decides to desert. Under the principle 'God has called us to peace' (v. 15), he argues that if an unbelieving partner desires to separate, the believer 'is not bound'. This so-called Pauline privilege is set alongside the teaching that if possible the marriage should be maintained because of its missionary opportunity (v. 16). None the less, if the unbeliever deserts, the believer is set free ('not enslaved', *dedoulotai*).[81] This must presumably mean 'set free to marry again', whether 'not bound' means 'not bound to the marriage bond' or whether it means 'not bound to celibacy' as some commentators have argued. 'Free to be deserted' makes nonsense of the paragraph.

In both these sections (vv. 10-11; 12-16), we find Paul affirming that a Christian should not take the initiative in dissolving his or her marriage. However, in neither case does he apply the principle of permanence in a legalistic way, where other considerations affect the marriage relationship. In particular, in the situation in which a Christian partner is divorced by the pagan partner, the former is set free to marry again.

Paul is not therefore giving an absolute ban on remarriage.[82] Indeed, his acceptance of the permissibility of remarriage in some circumstances may find support from 1 Cor. 7:25ff, in which he addresses the 'virgins'. While they should remain content in their unmarried state (because of the present circumstances) – and while Paul gives other examples of those who are to be content with their present circumstances (v. 27) – namely for those who are unmarried not to seek a wife, and for those who are married not to seek release – this is not a strict ruling which all must obey. Presumably the unmarried of v. 27 can include those whose marriage has been terminated by the death of one partner, and who are specifically allowed to marry again (v. 39). It is arguable that 'Are you free from a wife?' (7:27) can equally apply to those whose marriage has been broken by divorce. For these also, we can infer, remarriage is no sin (7:28), though we would expect Paul in his context to counsel against this 'in view of the impending distress' (7:26).

Furthermore, earlier in the chapter, Paul has expressed his concern (against the pro-celibacy faction in Corinth?) for those unmarried people overwhelmed with sexual temptation, but without the special gift of celibacy (7:7-9). To them he says it is better to marry than 'to be aflame with passion'. We may infer that his concern would also extend to divorced people in similar circumstances, for though some can – maybe should – interpret marriage breakdown as a call to future celibacy, this can by no means be presumed for all. Such reasoning would constitute further indication that Paul did not give an absolute ban on remarriage after divorce.

SUMMARY OF CHAPTER 4

1 The Pentateuchal laws on premarital intercourse, incest and adultery were framed to preserve the view that in marriage, a man and wife are united in what is intended to be an exclusive lifelong union.

2 The legislation of Deut. 24:1-4 is the recognition of a permission (not prescription) for divorce, and gives legal conditions designed to reduce hasty divorce and minimize cruelty to the divorced wife. It thus recognizes the fact of marriage breakdown, and acknowledges the need for societal legislation to regulate divorce.

3 Post-exilic writers reaffirm the divine intention for the permanence of marriage.

4 Divorce is never encouraged or commanded in the Old Testament.

5 The Synoptic divorce material reflects the Pharisaic dispute about the interpretation of the Pentateuchal legislation. In Jesus' day, the death penalty for adultery was not enforced. Gentile readers under Roman law would, like Jews, have assumed that divorce following adultery was legally required.

6 In the Synoptic material, Jesus reaffirms the divine law for the permanence of marriage, and brings divorce-with-remarriage under the seventh commandment against adultery.

7 Matthew's *porneia* clauses (meaning 'unlawful sexual intercourse')

are most satisfactorily seen as expounding the significance of Deut. 24 in the context of Jesus' day, and as indicating the continuing need for societal legislation to regulate divorce because of 'the hardness of men's hearts'.

8 The primary emphasis in Jesus' teaching, however, is that in the will of God for marriage, divorce has no place, and to initiate the 'putting away' of one's spouse infringes the commandment against adultery.

9 In the teaching of Paul, we find the same two emphases: the law of God for the permanence of marriage, and the recognition that there are circumstances is which it is important to legislate for exceptions.

10 Both Testaments indicate that when divorce occurs (however wrongly), right of remarriage is presupposed; in other words, when a marriage has been broken, divorce dissolves the marriage 'bond' and covenant; the Bible does not know legal separation without the possibility of remarriage.

REFERENCES TO CHAPTER 4

1 G. J. Wenham, *Marriage and Divorce: The Legal and Social Setting of the Biblical Teaching* (a Memorandum submitted to the Church of Ireland Committee on the remarriage of divorced persons). A summary appeared in *Third Way* Volume 1, Nos 20-22 (1977).

2 Wenham, *op. cit.*, p. 8; *Third Way*, 1/21, p. 7f.

3 *Ibid.*

4 Wenham, *op. cit.*; *Third Way*, 1/21, p. 8. However, Wenham also adds: 'These laws seem to be based on the principle that the act of sexual intercourse creates a relationship which ought to be made public in lifelong marriage.' Here there is an ambiguity: it appears that Wenham means that the act of intercourse in itself *creates* the permanent lifelong union (described by the phrase 'one flesh') which cannot be broken – a view we have criticized earlier.

5 C. F. Keil and F. Delitzsch, *Biblical Commentary on the Old Testament*, volume 3 (The Pentateuch), trans. J. Martin (Eerdmans), p. 124.

6 Keil and Delitzsch *op. cit.*: 'upholds the sacredness of marriage'.

7 J. D. M. Derrett, *Law in the New Testament* (1970), p. 363f.

8 e.g. J. Murray, *Divorce* (1961), p. 5; Keil and Delitzsch, *op. cit.*,

volume 3, p. 416: 'In these verses . . . divorce is not established as
a right; all that is done is that in the case of divorce, a reunion
with the divorced wife is forbidden.' Cf, also S. R. Driver,
A Critical and Exegetical Commentary on Deuteronomy (T. & T.
Clark, 1895; ICC reprint 1951), p. 269. Cf. G. von Rad, *Deuteronomy* (SCM, 1966), p. 150.

9 J. Murray, *op. cit.*, p. 6.
10 *Ibid.*, cf. Driver, *op. cit.*, p. 272.
11 *Mishnah Ket.* 9.9, and presupposed through *Git.*
12 e.g. A. Isaksson, *Marriage and Ministry in the New Temple* (1965).
13 Cf. Driver, *op. cit.*, p. 271: 'immodest or indecent behaviour'.
14 Isaksson, *op. cit.*
15 Calum M. Carmichael, *The Laws of Deuteronomy* (1974), p. 203f.
16 *Ibid.*: 'the male concern with the public behaviour of women in
Mesopotamian society' is noted by reference to the Hammurabi
law No. 143: 'If she was not careful, but was a gadabout thus
neglecting her house and humiliating her husband . . .' quoted
from J. B. Pritchard (ed.), *Ancient Near Eastern Texts* (1969)[3],
p. 172.
17 F. Brown, S. R. Driver, C. A. Briggs, *A Hebrew and English
Lexicon of the Old Testament.*
18 Wenham, *Third Way*, *1/21*, p. 9, quoting R. Yaron, 'The Restoration of Marriage', *JJS*, *17* (1966), p. 1ff.
19 Derrett, *op. cit.*, p. 379, quoting J. Breslawi, *P. Korngruen Volume*,
pp. 44-56.
20 Cf. Driver, *op. cit.*, p. 272; cf. D. W. Shaner, *A Christian View of
Divorce* (1969), p. 36.
21 Wenham, *Third Way*, *1/21*, p. 9.
22 J. Baldwin comments: 'English versions agree that this is the
prophet's meaning, even though the Hebrew in fact reads "if he
hates send (her) away" . . . Evidently the text suffered early at the
hands of some who wanted to bring Malachi's teaching into line
with that of Deut. 24:1 which permitted divorce. Such a reading
undermines all that the prophet is seeking to convey.' *Haggai,
Zechariah, Malachi* (1972), p. 241.
23 Derrett, *op. cit.* Derrett does want to say that the 'one flesh' union
cannot ever be broken. He says that we are not at liberty to
interpret the Mosaic concession about divorce in a way that goes
against God's creation ordinance (the Moses of Gen. 2:24).
But that seems to be precisely what Jesus does in the dispute with
the Pharisees (see discussion).

24 *Mishnah Git.* 9.3.
25 Cf. Wenham, *op. cit.*, and *Third Way, 1/20*, p. 3f.
26 *Mishnah Git.* 9.10.
27 Philo, *De Specialibus Legibus* 3. 27.30.
28 Josephus, *Life,* sec. 2.
29 *Ibid.,* sec. 75, 76.
30 Josephus, *Antiquities,* 4. viii. 23.
31 *Mishnah Ket.* 7.6.
32 Wenham, *Third Way, 1/20*, p. 4.
33 *Babylonian Talmud Git.* 90b.
34 *Ibid., Ned.* 20b, quoted in the Editorial Introduction to *The Babylonian Talmud* ed. Rabbi Dr I. Epstein (1936), p. xxxiv.
35 Epstein, *op. cit.*, p. xxiv.
36 Derrett, *op. cit.*, p. 156ff. Cf. A. N. Sherwin White, *Roman Society and Roman Law* (1965).
37 L. M. Epstein, *Sex Laws and Customs in Judaism* (1948), p. 209.
38 *Mishnah Sot.* 5.1, cf. *Yeb.* 2.8.
39 *Ibid., Git.* 9.8. The Midrash on Num.IX.12, ed. H. Freedman and M. Simon (1939), reads: 'You have a type of person who, if a dead fly falls in his cup, takes out the fly, sucks it, and then drinks. Such is the wicked man who sees without protest his wife being intimate with her servants, going out into the market place with her head uncovered, garments slit on either side, and bathing in a spot where men bathe. A woman like this it is an imperative duty laid down by the Torah to divorce.'
40 Josephus, *Antiquities,* 15, vii. 10.
    Cf. C. E. B. Cranfield, *St Mark* (1955), p. 322; also W. D. Davies, *The Setting of the Sermon on the Mount* (1964), p. 462 quoting D. Daube, *The New Testament and Rabbinic Judaism,* p. 362ff.
41 *Mishnah Ket.* 7.9, 10.
42 *Ibid., Git.* 2.5.
43 *Arak.* 5.6; cf. *Yeb.* 14.1: 'The man that divorces is not like to the woman that is divorced; for a woman is put away with her consent or without it, but a husband can put away his wife only with his own consent.'
44 B. Nicholas, *Roman Law* (1962), p. 85f.
45 J. P. V. D. Balsdon, *Roman Women* (1962), p. 77f.
46 *Ibid.*
47 See for example D. Catchpole, 'The Synoptic Divorce Material as a Traditio-Historical Problem', Bulletin of John Rylands'

University Library of Manchester, 57, No. 1, Autumn 1974, and references cited.

48 Cf. here C. R. Fielding's comments in F. W. Beare, *The Earliest Records of Jesus* (1962), p. 190f; and D. Catchpole, *op. cit.*

49 e.g. D. L. Dungan, *The Sayings of Jesus in the Churches of Paul*, (1971), p. 122; A. Isaksson, *op. cit.*

50 'That which God has joined . . .' refers to the institution of marriage, and to the fact that the marriage covenant is part of God's work in creation. In other words, God ordained the institution of marriage, and wherever a marriage displays personal commitment, social recognition and legal regulation within the meaning of 'covenant', there the marriage can be said to be 'of God'. 'Those whom God has joined . . .', the personal reference in the Prayer Book Marriage Service, is a particularizing of the more general statement of the evangelist. It is none the less true, however, that for this particular man and this particular woman, now sharing in God's intention for marriage, God acts to 'join together' (in a way analogous to that in which we can properly speak of God's action in the creation of a new life at conception).

51 The primary reference is to the sin of Israel which required the regulatory permission of Deut. 24:1; cf. D. Hill, *Matthew* (1972), p. 280, F. Filson, *Matthew* (1960), p. 206. However, as Catchpole comments, *op. cit.*, p. 126, quoting H. Greeven, *NTS* (1968-9), p. 377f, Jesus' questioners are brought within his judgement: 'What did Moses command *you*? . . . With a view to *your* hardness of heart Moses wrote this commandment for *you*.' This cuts against any sense that divorce might be regarded as a privilege for Israel, as some rabbis held.

52 Catchpole, *op. cit.*, p. 126, and refs cited.

53 Banks argues that Jesus is here doing more than expounding the true meaning of Deut. 24:1: he 'is setting it in a context in which it no longer applies, except as a condemnation of those who refuse to accept the new state of affairs which has come into existence'. R. Banks, *Law in the Synoptic Tradition* (1975), p. 149f. While this may well be true as far as it goes, it by no means cancels the need for such legislation wherever society is characterized by 'hardness of heart'.

54 Mark 10:11-12.
   In Mark 10:12 there are several valiant readings. The three most

important are (i) 'If she, when she has divorced her husband, marries another, she commits adultery. '(ii) 'If a woman divorces her husband and is married to another, she commits adultery.' (Both of these situations refer to the action of the wife in divorcing her husband, which reflects a Roman legal assumption.) (iii) 'If a woman leaves her husband and marries another . . .' etc. (which could reflect the current Palestinian legal position). Most versions follow (i) or (ii), or a compromise like RSV.

55 Cf. E. Schillebeeckx, *Marriage*, p. 145, and commentators quoted. Cf. also Council of Trent, Session XXIV, Canons 7, 8.

56 Cf. e.g. Josephus, *Antiquities*, 15.vii.10; 18.v.5.

57 Cf. John Job, *Third Way*, *1/21*, p. 14.

58 Fielding, *op. cit.*

59 B. Vawter, 'The Divorce Clauses in Matt. 5:32 and 19:9', *CBQ, 16* (1954), p. 155-67; A. Isaksson, *op. cit.*, p. 127ff; E. Schillebeeckx, *op. cit.*, p. 147ff; D. Shaner, *op. cit.*

60 There is no MS evidence that it is a scribal interpolation; even the alternative reading of Codex Vaticanus (RSV margin) does not omit the clause in 19:9. Cf. Murray, *op. cit.*, p. 48ff. Most modern commentators accept the authenticity of the text, but regard the clause as an insertion by Matthew into the tradition which stems from Jesus (so *Marriage and the Church's Task*, and many commentators). This is by no means essential, however, and as Isaksson comments (*Marriage and Ministry*, p. 92), 'the disappearance of the clause in part of the transmitted material (referring to Mark 10), is probably easier to explain than its introduction into the Gospel of Matthew'. Certainly there is no tendency in Matthew's style to relax requirements of law, and it is difficult to see why he should have apparently done so here. The argument that the Matthean Church, faced with hard cases, here resorted to a casuistry is without parallel elsewhere in the Gospel.

61 Notes by C. R. Fielding in F. W. Beare, *The Earliest Records of Jesus* (1962), p. 190f.

62 *Ibid.*

63 Cf. J. Bonsirven, *Le Divorce dans le Neuf Testament* (1948), H. Baltensweiler, *Die Ehe in Neuen Testament* (1967). More recently Joseph Fitzmeyer S.J. in 'The Matthean Divorce Texts and Some New Palestinian Evidence', *Theological Studies*, *37* (1976), p. 197ff, has argued that the recently discovered *Temple Scroll* from Qumran contains evidence for the prohibition of divorce (and

therefore what he sees as Jesus' radical break with Palestinian tradition may not be quite so radical) and also that the *Damascus Document* may well give first-century Palestinian support for the view that *porneia* in the exceptive clauses in Matt. 5 and 19 refers to illicit marital union between persons of close kinship. 'Matthew therefore would be making an exception for such marital situations for Gentile Christians who were living in a mixed community with Jewish Christians still observing Mosaic regulations.'

64 *Marriage and the Church's Task*, p. 140.

65 Vawter, *op. cit.*

66 Isaksson, *op. cit.*; cf. Basil Atkinson's commentary on Matthew in *New Bible Commentary* (1953), F. Alwyn Adams, *Divorce* (1949); and most recently Mark Geldard, *Churchman 92*, no. 2 (1978), p. 134.

67 B. Malina, 'Does *Porneia* Mean Fornication?', *NT, 14* (1972), p. 10f.

68 Joseph Jensen, 'Does *Porneia* Mean Fornication? A critique of Bruce Malina', *Novum Testamentum, 20/3* (July 1978). Cf. also J. Fitzmeyer, *Theological Studies, 37* (1976), p. 208, n.44 which refers to Malina's treatment as 'oversimplified', and J. J. O'Rourke, *Theological Studies, 37* (1976), p. 478f which also disagrees with Malina's conclusions.

69 A. Mahoney, *CBQ, 30* (1968), p. 29ff.

70 D. Hill, *The Gospel of Matthew* (1972), p. 124.

71 Cf. e.g. J. Jensen, *Novum Testamentum, 20/3* (July 1978) and references cited.

72 The usage of *porneia* to mean 'adultery' can be illustrated from *LXX*: In Jer. 3, idolatrous Israel is pictured (v. 1) as the 'wife' of Jehovah. In v. 3, she is termed *pornes*, and in vv. 6-7 her adulterous conduct in going after lovers is *porneuo*. Ezekiel 16 employs the same picture: Israel's faithless consorting with the world is first described as fornication (*exeporneusas*), while in v. 39 her conduct is judged to be that of an adulteress (*moichalidos*). Cf. Hos. 3:1 (*moichalin*), 3:3 (*porneuo*). Likewise in Ecclus. 23:23, a wife who has had children by another husband is said 'in fornication to have committed adultery' (*en porneia emoicheuthe*). *Porneia*, therefore, often included adultery. (I am grateful to Canon J. Stafford Wright for these comments.) J. Jensen, *op. cit.*, argues that *LXX* uses *porneia* to designate all kinds of extramarital intercourse.

D. Shaner suggests that in the Sypnotic material, *porneia* would refer to 'persistent and unrepentant adultery', *op. cit.*, p. 80, though Banks argues that this gives the word a precision which it does not warrant. The correct term here would be *porne* or *porneiai*, whereas *porneia* does not refer to unchastity in general so much as to particular instances of it. *Op. cit.*, p. 155.

73 The view that the *porneia* clauses could be understood in an 'inclusive' rather than an 'exceptive' sense, is not now generally considered valid. On that view the phrase would read 'not even in the case of *porneia*'. Cf. Vawter, ref. 74.

74 B. Vawter, *CBQ*, *16* (1954), p. 155ff. This view is supported by R. Banks, *op. cit.*

75 Banks, *op. cit.*, p. 156n.

76 *Contra* e.g. Q. Quesnell, 'Made Themselves Eunuchs for the Kingdom of Heaven (Matt. 19:12)', *Catholic Biblical Quarterly*, *30* (1968) p. 335f. in which Quesnell argues that the calling to Christian marriage includes taking the risk that if a man and his wife ever have to separate 'he will be left for the rest of his life pledged to loyalty to one who is not even there'. To continue such faithful love, even when such love is not returned, is effectively to make oneself a eunuch – a person incapable of marriage for the rest of one's life. Quesnell thus argues from this verse that Jesus is ruling out all remarriage after divorce.

77 Rabbi Dr I. Epstein, Introduction to *The Babylonian Talmud* (1936).

78 Catholic commentators, arguing that Jesus is sanctioning separation only, and not divorce from the marriage bond, sometimes limit the application of the exceptive clause to *apoluo*. Murray *Divorce* p. 35f, argues that the clause applies to remarriage after divorce, as well as to the 'putting away'. He quotes C. Gore, *The Question of Divorce* (1911), p. 20: 'The exceptive clause in Mt. 19 which contains the words "and shall marry another" leaves no doubt that divorce is used in such sense as covers permission to remarry.'

79 Catchpole, *op. cit.*, p. 106.

80 Commentators do suggest, as we have seen, that the Matthean exceptive clause is to be understood as Matthean casuistry, but we have suggested an alternative explanation.

81 Cf. 1 Cor. 7:39 where *dedetai*, arguably a weaker word than *dedoulotai* (Murray, *Divorce*, p. 72ff), is used for the marriage bond.

82 Indeed, it is of interest that so definite an exponent of the absolute indissolubility of marriage as T. A. Lacey, sees a permission in this word of Paul for remarriage after desertion by a 'heathen partner'. He comments: 'It must be admitted that such an interpretation is inconsistent and irreconcilable with the principle that marriage is naturally indissoluble. It remains a curious and unexplained exception to the general rule.'

CHAPTER 5

Divorce and Remarriage

The Moral Questions

1. Covenant-Breaking

We have argued that the fundamental biblical description of marriage is that of covenant. This stands over against the view of marriage as an absolutely indissoluble *vinculum* in which divorce is impossible, on the one hand, and against the view of marriage as either a private contract or a romantic alliance terminable at will, on the other.

We have said that a covenant includes these four elements: (i) an undertaking of committed faithfulness made by one party to another (or by both to each other); (ii) the acceptance of that undertaking by the other party; (iii) public knowledge of such an undertaking and its acceptance; and (iv) the growth of a personal relationship based on, and expressive of, such a commitment. The covenant of marriage holds together the personal partnership of committed love and the publicly declared and publicly accepted responsibility of committed obligation. The 'one flesh' union in which the marriage covenant and sexual intercourse belong together, and which together form the basis for a new family unit, is a unitary partnership of faithful love which should not be broken and which cannot in fact be broken without damage to the partners concerned. It is this relationship which both reveals and is to be patterned on the relationship of the covenant God with his people. The marriage covenant is a life partnership in which permanence is not an ideal: it is a premise.

Jesus affirms this as the will of God for marriage in his reference back to the purpose of God in creation, in the Pharisees' dispute with him concerning divorce. 'What God has joined together, let no man put asunder' (Matt. 19:6; Mark 10: 9). St Paul likewise affirms this will of God for marriage in his insistence that 'a wife is bound to her husband as long as he lives' (1 Cor. 7:39), that 'the wife should not separate from her husband' and 'the husband should not divorce his wife' (1 Cor. 7:10-11). This 'law of God for marriage', rooted in creation (i.e. in what men and women are; Gen. 1:27; 2:24) includes the fact that the marriage covenant is a life-union, entered into as such by the partners and recognized as such by society.

However, the references to divorce in both Old and New Testaments also realistically admit that marriages are in fact broken. The Deuteronomic legislation, without advocating divorce, acknowledged that it occurred, and sought to restrict (by requiring adequate grounds: 'some indecency') and regulate it (by certificate) in a humane way (putting a curb on male cruelty and offering protection to the wife who might otherwise suffer such cruelty). Jesus also acknowledged the fact that through sin men can thwart God's intention. 'Let not man put asunder' admits the fact that man could. 'Whoever divorces his wife . . .' acknowledges that some do. Similarly, St Paul's 'Let not the wife separate . . . *but if she does* . . .' recognizes that there is a distinction between God's will and man's keeping of it. If marriage is understood in covenant terms, the dissolution of a marriage (though always outside God's will for marriage, and therefore sinful) is not thereby impossible. Covenants, although intended and entered into as committed and permanent undertakings, can be broken.

Once an undertaking is publicly expressed and accepted (and a covenant therefore exists), any unfaithfulness to it is in some sense a breach of the covenant. Such breaches may be secret (in the secret thoughts or intentions of one of the parties) or may be

openly expressed in attitudes, words or actions. While all
breaches are culpable in the sight of God (whether lustful looks
or physical adultery, for example), it is only when they are
expressed in such a way that they are known to the other partner
that the covenant is visibly affected and the need is created for
forgiveness and reconciliation between the partners if the
covenant relationship is to be maintained or restored.

So what does break the covenant of marriage? (Here we need
to keep clear the distinction between the internal personal heart
of the covenant relationship and its external social and legal
framework.) In its internal meaning, the marriage covenant is a
willing commitment to a permanent relationship, to committed
faithful love, to sexual exclusiveness, to the establishment of a
family unit of man and wife open to the possibility of parenthood. From this we argue that the internal aspect of the covenant, the heart of the marriage relationship, is therefore
threatened by an intention of the will to reverse the willing
commitment by which it was made. If such an intention is
expressed in attitudes, words or actions, the covenant is
breached and the relationship weakened or broken. Thus acts
of the will to refuse the commitment to sexual exclusiveness
expressed in breaking the 'one flesh' (by adultery or other
serious sexual sin); to refuse to remain faithful to the vow, the
calling, the person, the relationship of committed love (by
expressed attitudes or acts of cruelty, for example); to refuse to
maintain the family unit of man and wife together (by prolonged desertion, for example); all these strike at the heart of the
internal meaning of the marriage covenant. The commitment to
marriage was a commitment to contain whatever difficulties
arose within the marriage relationship. By an act of the will,
(expressed in attitudes, words or actions), an attempt can be
made to escape those difficulties by abandoning the relationship.[1] As O'Donovan comments:

This second act of will must always in principle be possible to us.
If it were not, it would mean that our acceptance of suffering was

no longer free and glad acceptance; it would be the accidental result of a decision taken many years before in ignorance of the future. When we bound ourselves into the structure of marriage we did not intend to renounce all moral responsibility for future suffering by means of one big decision that would settle it once and for all; we intended to accept the *support* that the structure offered for the continual exercise of our moral wills . . .

The perilous possibility remains that we can break our word. We break faith with our partner . . . we break faith with ourselves and with the institution of marriage . . .[2]

But this must be qualified, however, by stressing that not every act of the will which threatens the heart of marriage necessarily destroys it. Breaches of the covenant can be forgiven and healed. Nor, therefore, should a decision to abandon the relationship necessarily be thought irrevocable; nor does it necessarily lead to the public dissolution of the external covenant framework. On the contrary, to work in the covenant categories in which human marriage is to be patterned on the relationship of God towards his people, must always mean that the first response to unfaithful behaviour should be to seek and offer such forgiveness and reconciliation. We earlier stressed the emphasis in Hosea and other prophetic material, in particular, of the priority given to forgiveness, reconciliation and the restoration of broken covenants. The model of Christ's relationship to his Church displays and requires the same attitude.

However, where the will becomes so determined in its abandonment of the marriage relationship, by the refusal or spurning of forgiveness, for example, so that reconciliation and restoration become human impossibilities, or where the 'one flesh' is severed beyond healing by the habitual breach of the internal meaning of the covenant relationship, then the question of civil divorce (the public dissolution of the external covenant framework) arises.

Before we come to that question, however, we need first to ask how we are to view such abandonment of relationship from the perspective of the New Testament teaching which brings

divorce with remarriage under the heading of 'adultery'. What
is the Christian to say of the fact that some marriages have
never been – and some have ceased to be – the sort of relationships which display anything of God's will for marriage? How is
the Christian, seeking to be true to the moral principles of a
biblically informed faith to approach a situation, often tragic,
always painful, in which the will of man can and does thwart the
intention of God to the point at which it becomes humanly
impossible to find healing and restoration?

We must attempt to underline what some of these principles
are by returning to a discussion of the biblical material. In
particular we need to provide a basis for our discussion of civil
divorce by looking first at the relation between Jesus and Moses
on these issues.

2. Jesus and Moses

We begin with the fact that Matthew's first reference to the
question of divorce occurs in the Sermon on the Mount. In this
teaching to his disciples, Jesus is summarizing the character of
life appropriate for citizens of the kingdom of heaven (Matt.
5:3-12) and the influence of that character as salt and light in
the world (5:13-16). Matthew then recounts the teaching of
Jesus concerning his attitude to the Old Testament torah
(5:17), and what therefore the attitude of Jesus' followers
should be (5:19-20).

Christ's attitude to the Old Testament torah is not abolition,
but fulfilment (*plerosai*). 'Law' (torah) was a comprehensive
term for the total written revelation of God in the Old Testament scriptures,[3] and 'not an iota, not a dot, will pass from the
law until all is accomplished' (5:18).

The Sermon on the Mount gives an illustration of the
important place that the demand to 'do the Father's will'
occupies in the preaching of Jesus.[4] The entire passage (5:21-
48), including the reference to divorce (5:31-2), is a description
of the 'righteousness' which the disciples need in order to 'enter
the kingdom of heaven' (5:20), a righteousness which exceeds

that of the scribes and Pharisees. Jesus' ethic can therefore be described alternatively as an 'ethic of the righteousness of the kingdom', or an 'ethic of obedience to the Father's will'. The central emphasis in Jesus' teaching on love, to God and neighbour (Matt. 5:43f; 7:12; 22:36f, etc.) gives precise expression to what Jesus proclaims as the meaning of the law and the prophets (22:40), obedience to which conforms to the Father's will. Fulfilment of the torah and loving obedience to the Father thus become identified in Jesus. Furthermore, Jesus' own fulfilment of torah by his obedience to the Father's will, and the fulfilment he requires to be seen in the love of his disciples, is never merely prescriptive demand; it is also a gift. His fulfilment of torah, as his preaching of the Gospel, is an 'effective word' which *brings* those who will into relationship with the Father, and enables them to live within the Father's will.[5] In other words, righteousness is a gift, as well as a demand. It is in relationship with the Christ who fulfilled the torah by loving obedience to the Father that his disciples are enabled to live and love within the Father's will. To translate this into covenant categories (and with our understanding of covenant brought into clearest focus in the 'new' covenant in Christ's blood, cf. Matt. 26:28; Heb. 10:12ff), we may speak of covenant ethics as centering in the emphasis of the Gospel (righteousness given through the work of God's grace) which itself includes and fulfils 'torah' ethics (righteousness demanded in response to God's grace): 'I will be your God . . . you shall be my people.'[6]

From this background we can now comment more specifically on the so-called 'antitheses' of Matt. 5:21-48, which include the reference to divorce in 5:31-2. Several points need to be made.

First, Jesus' teaching is not set in opposition to the Mosaic law, but rather to the misinterpretation of it in the teaching of some of the Pharisees.[7] (Thus, Jesus does not quote what has been *written*, but what has been *said*, namely what the scribes taught the people orally. The tractates of the Talmud and the Midrashim mention the 'words of them of old' as a reference to

the learned rabbis. Furthermore, what Jesus quotes as 'having
been said' is for the greater part not found in the Old Testament
in this form; the quotations bear the marks of halachic instruction and interpretation, not of the law proper.[8] Then, in Matt.
15:2, Jesus explicitly mentions the 'tradition of the elders' and
contrasts God's law to it. The contrast in the 'antitheses' is not
only to the content of what was said, but to the one who is
speaking: 'by them of old' in contrast to 'But I say unto you'.)
As W. D. Davies comments,[9] therefore, the words of Jesus on
divorce in Matt. 5:32 can 'in no way be interpreted as a radical
departure from the Law of Moses, but only as a radical interpretation of it'. The teaching of Jesus is not to be held anti-
thetical to the written law of the Old Testament, though it is
critical of the oral tradition; it is the full interpretation of the
former rather than its annulment.

Secondly, therefore, by declaring the Father's will and
describing the pattern of life appropriate for citizens of the
kingdom, Jesus' teaching affirms two further things. First, it
affirms in effect (as does the whole of the Sermon on the Mount
in one sense) that the people of God are not to be thought of as
a people defined by a civil law code (as was in part true when the
people of God were understood in national terms, and had
become to be believed as the whole truth by some of their
number). They are a people identified instead by their covenant
relationship with God: they are citizens of the kingdom of
heaven. As a consequence of this, Jesus refuses to be sidetracked by the legal externals which preoccupied some of the
Pharisees, and penetrates to the heart of the Father's will which
lay behind the very laws which 'them of old' had misinterpreted
and misused.

But what can this 'full and radical' interpretation mean with
reference to the specific question of divorce, in Matt. 5:31-2?

We recall that from 5:27f Jesus has been teaching that any
unfaithfulness which cuts against the principle of 'one flesh'
marriage – of heart as much as of deed – is a breach of the

commandment against adultery. The comment about divorce comes as a natural sequel: an illustration of the way the Deuteronomic reference to divorce can be misinterpreted so as to lead to a breach of the seventh commandment. It appears that Jesus is setting his own teaching in opposition not to Deuteronomy 24, but to the Hillelite interpretation of it expressed in Matt. 5:31. Whereas certain of the Pharisees had come, through misuse of Deut. 24, to regard the meaning of marriage only in terms of its external structure (in which the question of grounds and procedures for divorce had become a preoccupation), Jesus refuses to be sidetracked by such detail (a divorced woman must be given a certificate) and affirms the will of God for the marriage relationship in which all reference to divorce comes under the heading of adultery. Jesus is not therefore criticizing the Mosaic rulings of Deut. 24. He is emphasizing instead that even behind those rulings there lies the will of God for marriage (and so the positive meaning of the divorce certificate legislation was to safeguard marriage against irresponsible dissolution by restricting and regulating divorce in a humane way). All divorce comes under the heading of adultery, and for those who live within the Father's will, the question of divorce legislation should not have to arise, let alone be put to the negative use exemplified by some Pharisees.

The same conclusions follow from the other Synoptic references to divorce. In Matthew 19, the primary emphasis again is the will of God for marriage (19:4-6). The Pharisees, believing that Jesus can be interpreted as criticizing Deuteronomy 24, then refer to the divorce certificate. Can they trap Jesus into a denial of what was indisputably written in the torah? Jesus, however, acknowledges that this regulation has a necessary place, but its necessity is because of sin ('hardness of heart', in which the Pharisees who sought to justify easy divorce also shared!), and it is God's concession rather than his intention. The purpose of Deut. 24, Jesus continues, is not to provide grounds for divorce, but to safeguard marriage by restricting and regulating divorce. It is marriage which is God's purpose (19:8b). Indeed (19:9), any divorce is a breach of God's will for marriage declared in creation and also in the seventh commandment, and so is tantamount to, or constructive of, adultery.

The only qualification to be made to the Matthean material concerns the *porneia* clauses which, we have suggested, are probably to be understood in an 'exceptive' sense (perhaps simply meaning that if one spouse has broken the 'one flesh' by *porneia*, the other does not break the 'one flesh' by using civil divorce proceedings on that account), and so refers to the need in a sinful society for civil legislation to regulate divorce.

In Mark's account (ch. 10), the dispute is set around the legitimacy of divorce at all. Here in stark absolutes, Jesus turns that question into the question of the will of God against which all divorce is to be measured. But by referring to divorce and remarriage as adultery, Jesus does not say that divorce cannot happen; rather that when it does, it breaks God's law.

The context in Luke's Gospel is different again, although here (16:18) the primary function of the divorce material appears to be as an illustration of what is involved in a return to the true meaning of torah. The whole section of the Gospel from 15:1 through to 16 is emphasizing the point that Jesus has come to do something about sin (15:1ff) and call men to repentance (15:7, 10). This is to involve the Pharisees as much as anyone else (15:2). The three parables of Chapter 15 serve as calls to repentance, and (if Derrett's exposition is accepted)[10] the point of the parable of the steward in 16:1ff is precisely whether the steward will keep the letter of his law code (albeit wrongly interpreted), or will serve God with his heart and so fulfil the meaning of the law. It is a calling back to holiness of character. Jesus then turns to the Pharisees and makes the same call to repentance applicable directly to them, for God knows their hearts (16:15). While they murmur against Jesus having dealings with sinners (15:1), the law which they claim to uphold stands to condemn their impenitence. Their exalting of things which are an abomination in the sight of God (16:15) is to be seen in the context of the coming of the kingdom (16:16), in which the law is not made void (16:17), but rather its meaning is deepened. The question of divorce acts as a precise illustration of this point. Luke includes it here to demonstrate the way in which the presence of the kingdom exposes the deeper meaning of torah. The way the Pharisees were using the law (as an authority to justify easy divorce) was an 'abomination' in the sight of God. Jesus affirms the inner meaning of that law (as a declaration of and buttress to the will of God for marriage), and thereby calls his hearers to repentance, a call which the following parable of Dives and Lazarus vividly illuminates (16:19ff). In other words, Luke's emphasis is on the purpose of God for godly character, on the offer of his grace, and on the fact that failure to live by his word is sin.[11]

3. Six Principles

On the basis of the above discussion, the following principles seem the most significant as basis for a Christian view of divorce in our contemporary society.

(a) In the teaching of Jesus we must *reject any antithesis between an 'ethic of law' and an 'ethic of disposition'*: both belong together within 'covenant ethics'.[12] The disposition of the heart is indeed a central part of the meaning of righteousness as Jesus preaches it, but it is required as such in the torah itself (Deut. 6:5, for example). Jesus emphasized the necessity for right attitudes in a disciple seeking to do the Father's will. But this did not cancel the meaning of torah, nor the need for civil legislation. It rather penetrated to the internal significance of the law alongside its external application. 'The disposition of the heart . . . is not some attribute transcending the law, but is subject to the law and demanded by the law. This appears nowhere more clearly than in the summary of the whole obedience which Jesus demands, viz. in the commandment of love.'[13]

Jesus certainly affirms that the people of God are not to be defined by externals (people subject to a specific code of civil law), but by their characters as people in covenant relationship with their God, citizens of his kingdom, obedient to their Father's will. But that does not negate the divorce regulations which were themselves part of torah, and behind which we can also see the command of God. The particular ruling on divorce in Deut. 24 is therefore in itself an application of the general meaning of marriage expressed in Gen. 2:24 and in the commandment against adultery.[14]

The ethics of Jesus do not take us out of the realm of torah (Fatherly instruction: the demand of righteousness in response to his grace). They do, though, penetrate to the deeper meanings within the torah (the dispositions of the heart), as well as emphasizing the further dimensions of the gift of righteousness made available through the work of grace. What God requires, in Christ he also gives. But to this we shall return shortly.

(b) *The 'Father's will' for marriage has a general validity for all men.* The ethical teaching of Jesus removes all limitation from the sphere of validity of divine law. In contrast to those who defined the people of God by nationality, Jesus' teaching is addressed to all men ('every one who . . .'). By referring back to Genesis and the creation narratives in his dialogue with the Pharisees on divorce, Jesus demonstrates that his teaching applies not just to Jewish (or Christian) marriage, but to human marriage in its totality.[15]

> The implication is that God does not have different marriage standards for Christians and for non-Christians. Marriage is one of his gifts to all men, not just a private arrangement for the benefit of the Christian community.[16]

In our discussion of A. T. MacMillan's proposal[17] for a double standard of marriage (those solemnized in church with the declaration of permanence, which should be regarded as indissoluble, and those solemnized before a registrar, which would not be regarded by the Church as indissoluble), we recalled that such a view has never been upheld by either Church or State. And the reason lies in the doctrine of creation to which Jesus specifically refers his teaching on marriage and divorce.

(c) *The Messianic 'gift of righteousness' provides the possibility for the fulfilment of the Father's will.* Jesus' teaching and his life are a unity. By his life he fulfilled the law in loving obedience to the Father's will. And, as we have said earlier, his fulfilment of the law is also *action, gift.* Christ's Gospel is an effective word which creates the relationship between the child and the heavenly Father, and through which 'righteousness' becomes the gift of a right relationship with himself through Christ. This gift includes the fulfilment of that promise of the covenant by which God will write his law in the hearts of his people (and thus enable its fulfilment). Or, put another way, includes the gift of the Holy Spirit, to the children of God 'who is not only the secret of their moral strength but of their entire spiritual existence, of their search for the kingdom of heaven, of their trust in the Father's love, of their discernment of his will and their expectation of the coming salvation, in short, of all that they need in order to live as children of the Father'.[18]

This point needs to be stressed in relation to God's will for marriage. If obedience to God's will is a gift belonging to the people of the kingdom, by which he makes them different human beings, writing his laws in their hearts, then because of this, obedience to the Father's will can be effectively asked,[19] and can become a reality in experience. Part of that gift is the relationship of the committed love of the Father to us through Christ, his forgiveness and his restoration, his concern and enabling for personal welfare, and all the ingredients which translated into human marriage terms make for the sort of marriage relationships which declare the meaning of God's covenant with us.

The same reasoning underlies the discussion on marriage in Ephesians Chapter 5. It is to a people who have been blessed in Christ with every spiritual blessing (1:3ff), been saved by a gift of God's grace (2:8f), become a dwelling place of God in the Spirit (2:22) and in whom the power of God is at work within (3:20), that the Apostle urges: Lead a life worthy of your calling (4:1), be imitators of God as beloved children (5:1), be filled with the Spirit (5:18), and express that life of the Spirit in being subject to one another (5:21). Then (5:22ff) expound the life of the Spirit in the context of marriage: the wife to 'be subject to her husband as to the Lord'; the husband to 'love his wife, as Christ loved'.

This does not imply that all marriages between those who do not profess faith in God through Christ thereby display nothing of God's will for marriage; on the contrary, when they do, they thereby (without perhaps recognizing the fact) demonstrate something of God's grace. Nor does it imply that all Christian marriages ideally follow the divine pattern. But it does imply at least the following three things. First, that marriage relationships which display before the world God's will for marriage by displaying the nature of his covenant, are the fruit of the work of God's grace, or what Helen Oppenheimer in her book *The Marriage Bond*[20] calls 'the harvest of the Spirit'. Secondly, that a marriage will be able to cope with failure to conform to the divine ideal, if it can learn from Christ what forgiveness, repentance and renewed obedience to the Father's will should mean. As we noted in our reference to the marriage covenant in Isaiah, it is the suffering servant of ch. 53 who is the agent of the restored covenant in ch. 54. Thirdly, such a 'harvest' can be refused, the Holy Spirit can be 'grieved' (Eph. 4:30), sin is still a reality, and covenants are broken. But where, as we noted when discussing the views of Augustine, there is a response of the marriage partners to the love of Christ, where there is an ordering of life under his redemptive grace, the strengthening factors are available which point towards and sustain the ideal of indissolubility and by which that ideal can become a reality.

(d) *We must be careful not to interpret the teaching of Jesus as a*

new law code by which the Father's will is achieved. Covenant
ethics hold together both the declaration of the Father's will in
his law, and the harvest of his Spirit by which it may be obeyed.
And in criticizing the legalism of some Pharisaic understanding
of marriage, we must beware of using the teaching of Christ in a
legalistic way. This is not to say that Jesus did not give commands, nor that his commands need not be obeyed. As Helen
Oppenheimer comments: 'It has frequently been insisted that
"Christ did not legislate", but to put the matter so can be mis-
leading, if it is then assumed that Christ's commands need not
be obeyed. Christ was not accustomed to pronounce upon a
man's rights: he propounded a better way in which God's will
would be done and questions about rights could remain un-
asked.' But Christ's pronouncement on the question of
divorce was in particular directed against the confusion of the
inner relational meaning of marriage with its external legal
aspect,[21] by which the whole question of divorce had become
obscured in rabbinical legal formalism. Dooyeweerd adds to this
point 'It is nothing but a relapse into this legalistic view of the
matrimonial bond if one tries to derive from the New Testament
legal principles for a civil law regulation of the grounds of
divorce'.[22] It would be clearer if he said that the New Testament
does not offer a code of law for civil divorce legislation (because
as we shall argue, certain New Testament principles *are*
relevant to the question of civil divorce law). But the main
point stands: that we miss the mark if we use the teaching of
Jesus (the 'exceptive' *porneia* clause, for example) either to
justify easy divorce, or to suggest that any not guilty of *porneia*
have thereby fulfillled the Father's will for marriage.

(e) *The New Testament speaks both of the Father's will and of his
concessions because of sin*. By referring to creation ('from the
beginning it was not so'; Matt. 19:4; Mark 10:6), and by bringing divorce under the heading of the seventh commandment
(Matt. 5:32), Jesus proclaims the Father's will for marriage. By
not rejecting the Mosaic ruling to regulate divorce, but regard-

ing it as a concession because of 'hardness of heart' (Matt.
19:8), though none the less part of the law of God (the giving of
a certificate was a 'commandment', Mark 10:5), and by his own
words ('Every one who divorces . . .'; 'Let not man put asunder'),
Jesus recognizes that the Father's will may be thwarted by sin,
and that social regulation of divorce therefore becomes necessary.

St Paul likewise distinguished between the will of God for
permanence and the need for specific rulings if that will was not
adhered to. The affirmation of the law of God for marriage
cannot therefore be taken to imply that there is no place for
legislation to regulate divorce within a sinful world. As H.
Thielicke puts it, referring to Jesus' words:

> His challenge is rather a call to repentance . . . a calling to re-
> membrance of God's 'real' order of creation.[23]

The effect of Jesus' reaffirmation of the 'real' will of God is
not to eliminate but to 'relativize'[24] the (necessary) legal
structures of this present age.

It has been the consistent view of theologians of the Reformed tradition (exemplified most clearly in Reformation
times, perhaps, by Peter Martyr), that Christian thinking on the
subject of divorce needs to hold two principles firmly together:
the permanence of the marriage covenant in principle and
divorce as a tragic, but real, exception. The essential moral
force of Jesus' affirmation of the will of God for marriage
implies the following principles. First, that the permanence of
marriage is not merely an ideal. Marriage is in fact a covenant
in which permanence is not only possible, but indeed is part of
the very meaning of what covenant is about. Secondly, divorce
must therefore always be seen as sin or the result of sin,
involving social evil as well as personal tragedy. As Cranfield
comments in his discussion of Mark 10:5

> Human conduct which falls short of the absolute command of
> God is sin and stands under divine judgement. The provisions
> which God's mercy has designed for the limitation of the con-

sequences of man's sin must not be interpreted as divine approval for sinning. When our sinfulness traps us in a position in which all the choices open to us are evil, we are to choose that which is least evil, asking for God's forgiveness and comforted by it, but not pretending that the evil is good.[25]

(f) *We are not, therefore, to place the covenant ethic of the law of love which fulfils the Father's will over against the juridical sphere of civil legislation.*[26] It is true that Jesus does not point to God's demand by way of civil law. It is true also that he demonstrates that those who determine their ethical attitude as to what is possible and permissible by virtue of civil legislation (as apparently was true of the Hillelites with the divorce certificate), 'shirk God's radical demand with respect to their lives'.[27] But Jesus does not take sides against the civil order as such, and his reference back to creation (and so to a context which does not presuppose man's sin) does not cancel the law given to restrain sin.

> Jesus does not reject these ordinances as such for they have been given to restrain sin and not to allow it . . . but he rejects that application and appeal to them which tries to escape from the real and original divine demand.[28]

For what purposes then is civil divorce legislation to be framed?

In our discussion of Deuteronomy 24, we suggested that the law served to restrict easy divorce by requiring adequate grounds, to regulate its practice and so to protect the wife and put a curb on male cruelty. In his acknowledgement of the need for such legislation because of 'the hardness of men's hearts', Jesus appears to endorse such purposes. This is another way of saying that Jesus endorses the function of law in the preservation of human society in order and justice.

The Reformers used to speak of the threefold functions of the law of God.[29] In his small book *Christ's Strange Work*, A. R. Vidler restated this threefold function: first, God has ordained laws and authorities to administer them, in order that human society, man's common life may be preserved, and prevented from breaking up into chaos or anarchy;[30] secondly, God by his law summons us to repentance;[31] thirdly, God's law shows the regenerate the path that they should walk in, and warns them whenever they are straying from it.[32] We have seen how St Luke in particular referred to God's law for marriage as part of a calling to repentance. The main thrust of Jesus' teaching on marriage shows 'the regenerate the path that they should walk in'. But in the matter of civil divorce legislation we are primarily concerned with the first function of law: the preservation of human society in order and justice. Vidler goes on to say that in this preservative function, God's law in the Old Testament 'lays down the basic conditions which must be observed if there is to be a tolerable and wholesome form of existence for human society'. He goes on to find this function of law in Paul's words to Timothy in 1 Tim. 1:8-11, and adds

> This passage shows that the use of the law for the restraint or suppression of evil is not only an Old Testament idea, nor is it St Paul's private opinion. It is part of the glorious Gospel that had been committed to him. It is the Gospel which obliges Christians to take politics and social legislation seriously.[33]

But more than simply restraining sin, in our society civil law has a normative function in shaping attitudes and promoting certain actions while restraining others. While civil legislation does not itself produce godly character, it can provide conditions which facilitate its growth.[34]

Drawing these points together in the context of our discussion of divorce, therefore, we conclude that civil divorce legislation needs *first* to provide a context in which covenant love in the marriage relationship can flourish and be maintained: in which the harvest of the Spirit can grow (and therefore should provide sufficient barriers to easy divorce that divorce is never a first option, but always the tragic last resort); *second*, to provide for the maximizing of support and aid in reconciliation for the hard times; and *third*, to regulate the ways in which marriage covenants may be terminated in line with the principles of order and justice.

4. Divorce

In attempting to apply these principles to our contemporary situation, three particular issues call for further comment.

(a) Divorce is a moral act

The condemnation of Jesus is directed against those who take the initiative in 'putting away' their spouse. To speak in covenant terms underlines the fact that although marriage is entered into as a life partnership, marriage relationships can be broken by the will of the partners, and the external framework of covenant can be dismantled by civil decree. Covenant categories require acknowledgement of responsibility for sin. Covenants do not just 'break down', they are broken; divorce expresses sin as well as tragedy. To be sure there are many difficult situations in which many minor 'offences' on both sides drive a relationship gradually to breaking point, and indeed any specific 'offence' may well be the symptom of a deeper failure in fulfilling covenant obligation. But from a biblical moral perspective, we cannot dissolve the category of 'matrimonial offence' without remainder into the less personally focused concept of 'irretrievable breakdown' (accepting, however, that from a legal point of view, the latter may well have certain advantages, at least theoretically).

From this standpoint we have to criticize the way in which the Root Report, *Marriage, Divorce and the Church*, explored the question whether marriages can 'die' (which would give a new meaning to 'till death us do part'). The authors affirmed that, just as some within the Eastern Orthodox Church suggest that 'moral' as well as 'physical' death can break the marriage bond,[35] so it was important to discover whether there was a moral consensus within the Church of England 'that some marriages, however well-intentioned, do break down'.[36]

In contrast to the Eastern Orthodox insistence that the 'permission for divorce in no way denies the tragic and sinful nature of every marriage breakdown',[37] the Root Report (and indeed much of the way 'irretrievable breakdown' is currently understood) appears to transfer all question of blame for divorce away from the partners and to the 'marriage', as though (as D. Field comments) 'the institution of marriage can be made into some kind of third party scapegoat on which all guilt can be laid'.

> If the marriage itself is to blame, why should the partners feel in any way guilty as individuals? . . . In so far as they are involved at all, the couple are cast as the helpless victims of circumstances: psychologically accident-prone, perhaps, in the difficult business of making relationship, but no more to blame than anyone who labours under a handicap.[38]

Furthermore, and particularly when the institution of marriage and the family are coming under criticism from a certain strand of psychological thinking,[39] we need to beware of dissolving the question of personal responsibility for making choices and keeping promises into a convenient sort of psychological or institutional determinism. The latter may serve as targets for blameshifting (and indeed, this is not to deny a measure of psychological or institutional pressure in the breaking of some marriages), but a denial of personal responsibility is ultimately a denial of an important part of what it means to be human.

The covenant model for marriage places the question of divorce in the area of moral responsibility. The theology of the 'absolute indissolubility of marriage by natural law' seems to deny the above affirmation that men can and do choose whether or not to remain faithful to their covenant obligations. To argue that divorce is impossible is neither biblically warranted nor pastorally realistic. God's law for marriage is a moral law, and therefore it is possible to conceive of exceptions on the basis of some other moral considerations. To see divorce as a moral question thus allows a way of handling situations of moral offence without pretending that some metaphysical relationship exists whatever moral choices we make and however irreparably broken in practice relationships may become. It does not, however, minimize the responsibility of the partners – and of society – before God to be answerable for the way the moral obligations for the permanence of marriage are handled.

Two further points must be made, the first of which we shall elaborate in the next section. First, breaches of covenant may be grave (like physical adultery, which specifically denies the 'one flesh'), or may be relatively trivial (like the wrongful expression of a bad temper). Although both alike create the need for forgiveness and reconciliation, they do not equally threaten the continuance of the covenant and raise the question as to its dissolution.

Secondly, in biblically informed morality, persistent and unrepentant sin is one thing; the action which, though of itself not morally good may none the less be right in the circumstances (like bearing arms in war), is quite another. We need to maintain a similar distinction in discussing divorce. We need to distinguish between those who through wilful sin will not live the life of a committed partnership of love, and those who, for a variety of possible reasons, are – despite their own desire to do so – unable to live that life. In other words, although legally and socially in institutional terms all 'divorcees' are identical in that they were once married but are married no longer (and indeed the Church needs to recognize all civil decrees, even those granted on what from a theological standpoint it may regard as trivial grounds, as *de facto* divorces), in theological and pastoral terms this identity of 'divorcees' is not adequate.

While the condemnation of Jesus ('He who puts away his wife') and Paul ('the husband should not put away his wife') against the deliberate breaking of marriage is unambiguous ('Let not man put asunder'), there are situations in which a partner, fully desiring to honour covenant obligations undertaken in a marriage, is none the less unable to, and can responsibly (though regretfully and repentantly, and only as a last resort) consider whether to ask the court to recognize and declare that the marriage has been broken. Thus John Murray, for example,[40] in his exposition of the binding nature of the 'basic law of marriage' in Rom. 7:2-3, none the less conceives of 'the woman as being relieved from this law of her husband by some kind of action for which she has no responsibility, but which involves a complete dereliction of fidelity and desecration of the sanctity of the marriage bond on the part of her husband'. A woman, in other words, all attempts at reconciliation with her adulterous husband having failed, could not be held to violate the law of marriage herself if she asked for public recognition (by the divorce court) that the marriage had been broken (by the husband). Now whereas Murray finds such a 'dereliction of fidelity' only in the act of adulterous intercourse (basing this on Matt. 19:9), we have suggested (and shall argue more fully shortly) that any action which constitutes unfaithfulness to the marriage covenant so persistent and unrepentant that reconciliation becomes impossible may be sufficient to break the bond of marriage and so may release the other partner from their covenant promise.

Although, therefore, in many breakdowns, the question of guilt or innocence is by no means clear cut, in moral (and pastoral) terms, a distinction needs to be made between relative unwillingness and relative inability to keep covenant, and the question of repentance before God will not necessarily be framed in the same terms for each partner.

(b) Divorce as the 'lesser evil'

The civil process of divorce is always tragic and it is always painful. It seeks to remedy one kind of unhappiness by almost invariably creating another. Furthermore, we need to recognize that in a situation of marital failure there will often be several (sometimes conflicting) moral claims to be taken into account. Alongside the moral responsibilities of the partners themselves, and to each other, to which we referred under (a), there are wider considerations also. Not only (for the sake of the partners) is the marriage relationship intended to be permanent, but for the sake of society the marriage institution is required to be stable. All question of 'trial marriage' or 'serial marriage' would therefore cut against 'every human value that marriage stands for'.[41] Likewise, arbitrary divorce at the whim of either party could never be considered a responsible moral decision. Divorce by mutual consent would not necessarily (indeed would be unlikely to) take account of the wider obligations to family and society that the vocation to covenant fidelity implies. Having said that, however, Christian morality, seeking to find the way of 'righteousness' which attempts as far as possible to fulfil 'the Father's will' in a marriage breakdown situation of conflicting moral claims, when no course of action can be wholly good, can concede that responsible dissolution of marriage may sometimes be right in the circumstances. But even so, there are other moral factors to consider than just the concerns of the partners themselves.

D. O'Callaghan argues that since prejudice, emotion and personal interest will tend to distort the facts of the case, the possibility of divorce could only be considered a responsible course on the intervention of outside authority. He further argues that though in principle the State should be such an objective authority, the way State intervention works in practice is not satisfactory, tending in fact to undermine the whole meaning of marriage as a stable institution. He concludes therefore that dissolution of marriage by (in particular the Roman Catholic) Church authority alone is adequate for responsible intervention.[42]

However, precisely because God's law for marriage is for all men (and not just Christians), because the State is the instrument of God for maintaining the good and punishing evil,[43] and one of the functions therefore of civil law is to provide the context in which God's will may be done, it *is* the responsibility of the State to legislate for the institutional side of marriage (and it is therefore an important Christian duty to ensure that such legislation and its outworking are as just as possible).

O'Callaghan's primary point stands, however: namely that situations of marriage breakdown are properly the concern of others alongside the partners involved. That concern, we affirm, should be expressed in responsible civil legislation and court procedure.

Accepting the difficulties and complexities of moral choice, such concern can sometimes rightly be expressed in admitting responsible divorce. The complexities arise because of the difficulty in weighing the various moral values which the marriage covenant involves. From a Christian perspective such values must include (i) the welfare of the partners (their opportunity of growth to maturity emotionally and spiritually; their promise of lifelong support for one another in prosperity and adversity; their need for security in old age, and so on); (ii) the welfare of children (their emotional stability, maintenance, education, opportunities, security); (iii) the welfare of society (the local community; the Christian fellowship; the need for certainty of parenthood for children; the social need for stability of sexual relationships within a stable structure of marriage; the guarantee of equality to citizens, and so on).[44] The weighing of these and other values creates the further dilemma for the Christian:

> The very possibility of divorce, particularly when it takes the form of a threat to apply for divorce, often spells the end of a marriage where reconciliation would otherwise be possible.[45]

Such an attitude of threat is a denial of the teaching of Christ: He is for marriage and against divorce. However, as with all his laws 'he accommodates specific intentions to his deepest and most general intention: the well being of his children'. In this context, to ask for public recognition that a marriage has been broken, may be morally permitted 'if it is necessary to avoid a greater evil' (Smedes).[46]

Is it legitimate, then, to specify grounds on which it may be said that God disapproves of divorce less than he disapproves of its alternatives? Many Protestants have taken the Matthean *porneia* clauses (Matt. 5:32; 19:9), some adding the Pauline Privilege concerning the desertion of an unbelieving spouse (1 Cor. 7:15) as prescriptive legislation defining the only grounds on which divorce is permissible. Murray, for example, develops several detailed case studies based on the requirement of adulterous intercourse as the only Scriptural ground on which divorce is legitimate.[47] This would perhaps be valid if adulterous intercourse was believed to be of itself the only way in which the marriage bond was dissolved (other than death). However, apart from a few exceptions, Christians have not usually held that adultery itself dissolves the bond of marriage (with the corollary that the partners are obliged to seek divorce). Such an application of the *porneia* clauses is not, we have suggested, warranted exegetically, nor is it typical of the way Jesus normally gives moral teaching. Indeed, if we are right in bringing all the ways in which unfaithfulness to the marriage bond can occur under the heading of 'adultery', as Jesus seems to do in Matt. 5, to focus only on physical infidelity may hide many of the real causes of marital breakdown of which adulterous intercourse may be a symptom rather than a cause.

This is not to say that such adultery should not be regarded as the serious social crime and moral evil which the Scriptures describe it to be. Nor is it to say that adultery should not be seen as the primary reason for accepting that the marriage covenant has been broken. As Ramsey notes, 'Adultery as the primary reason for divorce appears to be the natural and just order of human relationships when claims, what is "due", are being considered.'[48] He goes on to say, however, that while different degrees of seriousness in the infraction of claims are of great importance, 'they give no ground for begging the question in Christian ethics in favour of divorce under one circumstance only, since divorce for any reason is absolutely different from no divorce at all'.[49]

Since the Deuteronomic legislation was framed largely to prevent cruelty, since the *porneia* clauses refer to unlawful sexual misbehaviour, since Paul seems to allow divorce as a result of desertion in some circumstances, such may well serve as paradigms[50] in clarifying the extreme seriousness with which the question of divorce should be approached, and in suggesting the sort of circumstances which might allow the moral permissibility of divorce as a last resort. Recognition of the persistent hardness of heart in an as yet still sin-affected society requires the recognition of the human impossibility of healing some broken relationships, and will allow divorce in extreme circumstances (but only with repentance) as the lesser evil. Such a course inevitably presses the question: 'Is it lawful to divorce one's wife for any cause?' The danger in framing the question that way is that we may lose sight of Jesus' answer to it.

(c) Divorce: the legal procedures

The previous section serves to underline the principles on which, we suggested, civil divorce legislation and court procedures should be based: First, to provide a context in which covenanted love-faithfulness can flourish and be maintained (and therefore to minimize the opportunities in which the temptation to 'threaten to apply for divorce' can arise and to provide barriers also against easy divorce); second, to maximize opportunities (and agencies) for reconciliation and support when marriages are in trouble; third, to regulate the ways in which society will tolerate the termination of marriage covenants so as to maximize justice and social stability. A Christian is thus rightly concerned both with the content of divorce legislation and with the operation of the courts, and this for two further reasons. In the first place, as Cranfield said[51] divorce 'stands under divine judgement', and the Christian may properly hear in the decree of divorce pronounced by the human judge the word of divine judgement against sin.[52] That invests the divorce decree with such seriousness that the operation of the courts must be a matter for Christian concern. Secondly, the Christian will be concerned with the social effects of divorce legislation: specifically the effect that law and court procedures have on the stability of marriage and of family life.

In Britain, the 1969 Divorce Act which became law in 1971 has undoubtedly contributed to the phenomenal increase in the divorce rate of recent years. That Act, giving effect to some of the recommendations of the Anglican Report *Putting Asunder* (1966), replaced the concept of 'matrimonial offence' by the sole ground of 'irretrievable breakdown' of the marriage. Before such irretrievable breakdown can be established, the petitioner must satisfy the court of one or more of the following facts: (i) that the respondent has committed adultery and the petitioner finds it intolerable to live with the respondent; (ii) that the respondent has behaved in such a way that the petitioner cannot reasonably be expected to live with the respondent; (iii) that the respondent has deserted the petitioner for a continuous period of at least two years immediately preceding the presentation of the petition; (iv) that the parties to the marriage have lived apart for a continuous period of at least two years immediately preceding the presentation of the petition and the respondent consents to a decree being granted; (v) that the parties to the marriage have lived apart for a continuous period of at least five years immediately preceding the presentation of the petition.[53]

Since 1971 there has been a steep rise in the divorce figures, and while accepting that a considerable proportion of decrees granted were simply regularizing marital breakdown situations in which divorce was not possible under the previous law, this cannot account for the whole of the continuously rising trend. It is natural, therefore, to question whether such legislation has helped or hindered the advancement of the Christian understanding of marriage. There are two distinct issues here, however, which should not be confused.

On the one hand, there is the effect of legislation on general social expectancies. To pass legislation which removes certain barriers inevitably makes the behaviour formerly barred more common, and gradually more acceptable. The more common divorce becomes, the more fragile becomes the social institution of marriage;[54] easy availability increases the demand for easy divorce. It is without doubt true that many of the social and legal factors buttressing marriage as a permanent partnership have been eroded, and it is arguable that the 1969 Act is part of such a trend.

On the other hand, it is not clear that the barriers removed by the 1969 Act were in fact necessarily upholding the Christian view of marriage as a covenant of committed love, although they did in theory provide conditions in which it could flourish. But, as Helen Oppenheimer suggests,[55] in a comment on the views expressed within the Church of England against changes in the divorce law: 'What the Church was trying to uphold was the indissolubility of marriage. What it found itself upholding was the matrimonial offence.' Now while 'matrimonial offence' is, we have argued, the right moral category by which to speak of divorce, legislation based on this category alone was, as is well known, open to severe abuse and injustice (in the need to prove or invent 'offences' in order to 'get a divorce'). This was not because the basis of the older law was necessarily wrong in itself, but because in a society in which adultery was no longer considered a disgrace, nor divorce as a disaster, its constant misuse called it into disrepute. The authors of *Putting Asunder* argued that the primary Christian concern in civil divorce legislation should not be to make divorce as difficult as possible, but rather to make the law as just as possible, recognizing that there can be no divorce without some damage and pain. To that end they recommended the replacement of 'matrimonial offence' as ground for divorce by 'irretrievable breakdown', and in theory at least, the resulting law could arguably have led to a more just situation.

In fact, however, a number of serious question marks have to be placed over the way the Act is working – primarily concerned with the actual operation of this law in the courts – which throw severe doubts on its adequacy, and suggest that the concept of justice has very largely in practice dissolved into that of 'misfortune'.

First, despite the retention of the notion of offence[56] as indication that the breakdown is irretrievable, the concept of 'irretrievable breakdown' is a difficult concept for the courts to try. As Judge Irvine put it, 'If the petitioner says that the marriage has irretrievably broken down, the court has in practice no means of gainsaying such evidence, once one of the five declared sets of facts has been proved'.[57] Further, there are ambiguous phrases in the wording of the five conditions. How many cases of adultery are required before they can be said to be 'intolerable' to the petitioner? What constitutes behaviour which can be proved 'unreasonable'? The courts, being bound to apply such subjective criteria have, under pressure of increasing numbers of applications, found that the standards of what is required to be proved to establish 'intolerable' adultery or 'unreasonable' behaviour have been considerably slackened.[58] Similarly, what constitutes 'separation'? Judge Irvine writes: 'The courts have frequently held that parties can be living in separate households, though ostensibly living under the same roof.'[59]

Furthermore, the two barriers to be crossed in the granting of divorce under the 1969 Act are increasingly ineffective. (i) The Act requires that a petition cannot be presented within the first three years of marriage, unless a court grants leave for an exception where 'exceptional hardship' or 'exceptional depravity' can be proved. 'Judges of recent years have been increasingly liberal in granting such leave.'[60] (ii) The Act requires that the solicitor acting for the petitioner shall certify that he has discussed the possibilities of reconciliation with the client. By the time the situation has reached the solicitor, however, all too frequently the possibility of reconciliation has long been passed.

Such unhappy consequences in the working of this Act may well justify Christians wondering whether in the long run it has in fact helped towards the more just society in this area that the authors of *Putting Asunder* were seeking.

One further development (in 1977), namely the introduction of 'special procedure' divorce by amendment of Matrimonial Causes Rules (1973), appears to have even more serious consequences. This 'special procedure', by which almost all divorces are now dealt with by submission of a written affidavit to the registrar, without the need for the parties to come to court (effectively 'divorce by post'), was introduced – as is common in framing Rules of Court – without Parliamentary debate or public discussion. The principal reason behind the change was financial (to save money in the civil legal aid fund). The result is that 'once the registrar has given his certificate that the papers appear to be in order and the facts proved, there is a perfunctory pronouncement of the decree nisi in open court. This is a proceeding which normally occurs in a totally empty court, and would appear an undignified charade' (Judge Irvine).[61]

Such a procedure not only loses any sight of the seriousness with which the word of the court judge speaks the word of divine judgement, it could also signal 'the first step down a road which may end in the total withdrawal of the judicial function from the divorce process'.[62]

5. Nullity

At this point it is necessary to recall that there is one long-standing Christian tradition which, holding firmly to the absolute indissolubility of a (valid and sacramental) marriage, and therefore outlawing all divorce (except in certain circumstances of dispensation), seeks to provide relief from intolerable marriages by a procedure of annulment. The medieval marriage law contained references to numerous impediments, the existence of which gave rise to the growth of dispensations and nullity suits, and so cumbersome and complex were the subtleties of law and the machinery of its administration[63] that the Continental Reformers set a severe limit to grounds of annulment and permitted divorce for certain limited causes.

The modern Church of Rome, which advocates the exploration of annulment after civil divorce in order to enable the partners to return to the sacramental fellowship of the Church, or to sacramentalize a second union, has of course a considerably more adequate approach to the question of annulment than that of medieval days. Indeed, there have been fairly radical changes of approach even in the last ten years.[64]

But the Church of England has not followed this route in dealing with marriage failures, and we judge, for good reasons. None the less this approach is being urged on the Church of England in some quarters, and we must give the question of annulment some attention here.

(a) English law

There are certain nullity situations already covered by English law. From the 'external' legal and social point of view, the marriage begins when the vows of consent are made before witnesses. In law there are three classes of circumstances in which the commitment made in the vows of consent may be terminated or avoided. There is the dissolution of the marriage contract by divorce, which formally terminates the marriage in law. And there are two classes of case which both come under the heading of nullity.[65] Whereas divorce is occasioned by some factor subsequent to the marriage vows being made, nullity refers to the circumstances or conditions prior to the purported marriage which made the contract in some way defective in law, such that no true marriage ever came into being.

The first of these classes is the 'marriage' which never really existed in law at all (and does not strictly require the intervention of the courts, except when the question of the legitimacy of any children is involved). Such a marriage is *absolutely void*. There are (since the Nullity of Marriage Act 1971) now only three grounds on which a marriage is void: (i) that it is not a valid marriage under the provisions of the Marriage Acts of 1949 and 1970 (that is to say, the parties are within the prohibited degrees of consanguinity or affinity, or either party is

under the age of consent, or the parties intermarried in dis-
regard of certain necessary formalities, such as failure to
publish banns or obtain a licence); (ii) that at the time of
marriage, either party was already lawfully married; (iii) that
the parties are not respectively male and female (in terms of
biological sex, not gender role, in those rare cases in which these
are not the same).[66]

The second class covers the marriages in which defects in the
making or performance of the contract enable the courts to
recognize it as null and declare it to be so. This is a *voidable
marriage*: a marriage made with lack of consent or lack of
capacity, but which remains legally binding on the parties until
a declaration of nullity is obtained. Since the Nullity of Marriage
Act 1971, there have been six grounds on which a marriage may
be voidable.[67]

1 Non-consummation, due to the incapacity of either party,
either through physical defect or some mental or moral dis-
ability which makes full intercourse impossible. This was the
only ground on which a voidable marriage could be declared
null until the Matrimonial Causes Act 1937, which introduced
the following five further grounds.

2 Wilful refusal to consummate. This marks a departure from
the principle that void or voidable marriages depend on defects
which existed at the time of the marriage contract being made,
and occasioned much controversy on that account, both in the
legal profession and in the Church of England. The Report of a
Commission appointed by the Archbishops of Canterbury and
York in 1949 (*The Church and the Law of Nullity of Marriage*,
SPCK, 1955), could not accept 'wilful refusal to consummate'
as a satisfactory ground for nullity and made representations to
the Royal Commission on Marriage and Divorce which was
then in session that wilful refusal to consummate the marriage
'ought no longer to be a ground for nullity',[68] and instead
should be regarded as grounds for legal separation or divorce.
However, according to M. Puxon, *Family Law* (1971)[2], this still
stands as part of English Nullity Law.[69]

3 Lack of valid consent, caused by duress, mistake, unsoundness of mind 'or otherwise'. Puxon comments: 'A person is regarded as being capable of giving consent if he is capable of understanding the nature of marriage, which involves a mental capacity to appreciate the responsibilities normally attaching to marriage.' Strong medical evidence would normally be required to invalidate a marriage on grounds of insanity. Proceedings on this ground must be instituted within three years of the marriage.

4 Mental disorder at time of marriage. 'If either party at the time of the marriage, though capable of giving a valid consent . . . was suffering from a mental disorder within the meaning of the Mental Health Act 1959, the marriage can be voidable, provided that such disorder made that party unfitted for marriage.'[70] Proceedings must again be instituted within three years.

5 Venereal disease at time of marriage (disease as defined by the Venereal Diseases Act 1971), and the petitioner at the time of the marriage was ignorant of the fact.

6 Pregnancy by another at time of marriage (often very difficult to prove).

(b) Theological considerations

Having outlined the law of nullity as it at present exists and which apart from wilful refusal to consummate has been acceptable to churchmen of all traditions, we must now turn to the central theological issue which the question of nullity raises. Are there circumstances in which the Church can decide that a relationship which society and even the partners themselves thought was a marriage, and was for a time lived as a marriage, was in fact in theological terms, never a marriage at all? Should the Church, in fact, have broader grounds for annulment than the State is prepared to allow? The Church of Rome says yes. In stressing the three elements of an indissoluble union, namely validity, sacramentality and consummation, the Roman Church believes that 'a union which does not possess these three qualities may be, in some sense of the word, dissoluble; or may be said not to exist'.[71] Through the work of Marriage Tribunals, the presentation of petitions, the hearing and sifting of evidence, the Roman Church seeks to establish on what grounds if any some marriages which have been legally terminated in a divorce court can be considered in theological terms never to have existed.

In his book *Marriage Annulment in the Catholic Church* (which according to the publisher's comment on the cover seeks to answer the questions: What makes a marriage legal in the eyes of the Church? On what grounds can a marriage be declared null and void? How do those who wish to have their marriage annulled go about it?), Monsignor Brown says that there has been a very radical alteration in the approach and starting point of Roman Canonists in the last few years. 'They no longer expect people to come along with claims of nullity to be investigated. What in fact happens is that people whose marriages have broken down come to a Tribunal and try to find out if there is anything that can be done to permit them to enter new marriages; or sometimes to see if an existing second union (contracted after the break of the first) can be sacramentalized in the Church.'[72] The Tribunal explores whether or not the marriage was invalid through lack of consent (which covers simulation of consent, total or partial; forced consent through fear, for example; defective consent, through ignorance of the nature of marriage, error of person, or inability to fulfil the obligations of marriage because of amentia, psychopathy, hysteria, etc; or because of lack of due discretion in severe immaturity). The Tribunal explores diriment impediments which make the marriage null or void by either divine law (e.g. consanguinity, affinity or impotence), or ecclesiastical law (e.g. being under age, certain crimes such as an adulterous partner's conspiracy to murder the spouse, certain legal relationships like adoption, being in Holy Orders, having taken solemn vows of the religious life). The Tribunal can also provide for dispensation in marriages which have not been consummated, and dissolution ('in favour of the faith': the 'Petrine Privilege') of marriages which are 'non-sacramental' because they were contracted with one of the parties not lawfully baptized.

There is clearly some overlap between the Roman Church law and English civil law, on the question of nullity, but the former goes considerably further than the latter. Its procedure turns on its understanding of marriage as absolutely indissoluble (if the consent is full and free, the union is consummated, and is 'sacramental' in the sense that it is between the baptized), and on the attempt to provide for cases of marital failure by presuming that if marriage has in fact broken down, there may well have been no 'true marriage' at all.

Much earlier Roman Canon law defined matrimonial consent in terms of the character of marriage as a procreative union. Since the Second Vatican Council, in which *Gaudium et Spes*[73] described marriage as a 'community of life and love' it has been proposed that personality disorder which renders a person unfit for married life, and half-hearted or inadequate consent, can be grounds for nullity.[74] Furthermore, there has been pressure to extend the Petrine Privilege, which made it possible to dissolve 'non-sacramental unions', to include dissolution of other valid and consummated unions of baptized people in other circumstances 'in favour of the faith'.[75]

How are we to assess the claim that some marriages, not voidable by civil law, may, so it is held, none the less theologically be regarded as nullities, in the light of our understanding of marriage not as an indissoluble sacrament, but as a covenant, and in the light also of the fact that the Church of England is encouraged by some to follow the example of the Church of Rome which while rigorously forbidding divorce affords relief to hard cases by deeming them to be nullities? This, says Bishop Chavasse,[76] was 'the real issue before the Nullity Commission of 1949', whose Report was published in 1955. That Report concluded that while the Church must be free to make a distinction between legal and canonical marriages and exercise its own discipline over its own members, in the question of nullity (with the exception of wilful refusal to consummate), it considered that the civil law (which was then the Matrimonial Causes Act 1950) was acceptable. The Commission further recommended that in any case where a person had obtained a divorce decree in a secular court, the Church should accept that decree as decisive even if it is subsequently suggested that a decree of nullity might have been obtained. There was, the Commission argued, no need for the establishment of Church Courts to deal with cases of alleged nullity.

The primary reason for this conclusion, with which we agree, is that the concept of Defective Intention can be, and is, stretched to such an extent that it renders divorce unnecessary. K. E. Kirk put the matter clearly (in what Chavasse called a 'polite but evident understatement') when he said

> There can be no doubt that the abuses of the nullity decrees of the Middle Ages have been in the main removed. But an uneasy suspicion lingers in many minds that nullity suits are still sometimes used as convenient substitutes for that divorce which Western Canon Law so stringently forbids.[77]

Or, as the more recent Report *African Christian Marriage* affirms, although the considerable widening of interpretation of the grounds of nullity (to include inadequate consent, or psychological incapacity) brings nullity procedures in some cases much closer to the actual causes of marital breakdown, 'there remains, nevertheless, the basic unwillingness to call a spade a spade'.[78]

Furthermore, from the covenant categories within which we believe it most appropriate to work, the public giving of vows of consent is the *terminus a quo* of what may properly be understood as a marriage, at least in its external and social aspects. Unless there is lack of valid consent in the terms already admitted in civil law, it seems nothing other than an evasion of the fact of divorce to suggest other than that where consent has been given, a marriage is brought into being. This is not to say that the legal framework creates the faithful commitment to the 'one flesh' bond which we have argued is the centre of the meaning of marriage. Nor is it to say that marriages cannot be destroyed. It is, however, to affirm that the understanding of the central meaning of marriage is brought into disrepute by the possibility that a person's marriage can be declared no marriage simply by saying that they did not really mean, or were not psychologically ready to keep the nuptial promises which they solemnly avowed in public.

But what are we to say, then, of the 'hard cases'? It is all too possible for two people, in haste or ignorance perhaps, urged on by the impulse of eros or the pressure of conformity (especially if the girl is pregnant) to go through a wedding ceremony. For some the words 'we made a mistake' are true before God. Are these 'marriages', theologically speaking? And what of the difficult concept of psychological inadequacy? Can this ever come within the theological understanding of nullity? On this Dr Dominian comments: 'One cannot offer in a contract something one does not possess, and that which is lacking can only be seen in the actual relationship, not before.'[79] And again, remarking on how the Pauline Privilege has been understood as indicating the need for a minimum spiritual relationship in a viable marriage, and how the medieval Church nullified marriages in which there was no physical relationship, he suggests that 'we have reached the stage' of recognizing the need for a minimum psychological and social relationship in a viable marriage.

> Seen in this light the task of the Church is to go on proclaiming the truth about indissolubility, the ideal of Christian marriage, and at the same time learn to distinguish what is viable from what is non-viable so that no marriage will be held to be so in the name of Christ which in reality cannot be.[80]

What are we to say of this?

The clearest way to handle these situations is to make again the distinction between the external framework of the marriage

covenant and its internal meaning as relationship. This enables
us to distinguish between good marriages (in which the external
is the framework for the internal) and bad marriages (in which
the former is but a hollow shell); and of course many gradations
between.

In the circumstances in which there is in fact lack of intention
in one or both partners to commit themselves to the inner
relational meaning of marriage, or where there is a refusal to
accept certain normative Christian obligations of marriage such
as parenthood, or if there is a deliberate reservation to condition
'permanence' by 'seeing how things work out', we might
properly from a theological perspective use the term 'defective
consent', and even consider these theologically speaking as
nullities. But to transfer such theological terminology to legal
and social contexts creates confusion. Vows are still vows (even
if inadvisedly made)[81] and if the vow is made, English law
rightly holds the contracting parties to their public consent as
against any private derogation of it. 'The parties are concluded
to mean seriously and deliberately and intentionally what they
have avowed in the presence of God and man, under all the
sanctions of religion and law.'[82] It is clearer and more in
keeping with the meaning of covenant to hold that bad marriages
are still marriages until dissolved by divorce, rather than suggest
that they have never been marriages at all.

Two further points need to be added. First, that bad marriages
can grow into good ones. Even if 'we made a mistake' is true
before God, the grace of God can enable the growth of covenanted lover faithfulness even within some marriage frameworks which began with inadvisedly made vows. But secondly,
if the marriage is and has only ever been the hollow shell of its
external framework, and there is no desire for, or willingness to
work at, the 'harvesting of the Spirit', or there is that inadequacy of which Dr Dominian speaks, the question of
divorce may properly arise. (That is not to say that divorce even
in such circumstances is necessarily the inevitable course; if
children are involved it may not be advisable.) But divorce, even

here, is no easy option. As Thielicke comments:

> Even from this point of view, divorce is always wrong, not indeed
> because the wrong lies in the act of divorce itself and therefore
> would become less heinous or not occur at all if the act were left
> undone, but rather because the act of divorce (in this case) is only
> a symptom of the condition of the marriage itself.[83]

That said, however, for the Church to refuse to recognize
divorce may cause it to become guilty of compounding sin
with confusion at best or hypocrisy at worst, by either insisting
on maintaining the shell of marital structure at all costs, or
declaring of no consequence vows which albeit inadvisedly were
solemnly and publicly made.

This throws a heavy responsibility on the Church and the
partners themselves in the question of marriage preparation. If
we are to minimize the (large?) number of bad marriages made
inadvisedly, lightly or wantonly, we must discover ways of
helping people before marriage to understand fully what they
are doing in the vows they make, and the resources that are
needed (and available) to sustain them in keeping them.

6. Remarriage after Divorce

Finally, what of the moral issues involved in the question of
remarriage after divorce?

The possibility, indeed likelihood, of remarriage after divorce
is presupposed in both Old and New Testaments, although, as
we have seen, a second marriage falls under the cloud of the
broken covenant of the first. It is arguable that St Paul was
intending to be dissuasive about remarriage, but he does not
give an absolute ban. A divorced person is no longer married,
the 'one flesh' has been severed, the external covenant framework has been dismantled and he or she is – in one sense – free
to marry again. But only in one sense, because several important
qualifications must immediately be added. The primary moral
question is whether or not remarriage cuts across any outstanding covenant obligations of the first marriage which are

capable of fulfilment. If there is any remaining possibility of reconciliation to the first partner, that is decisive. K. E. Kirk, while admitting the separation of two partners as a 'necessary evil if life together has become intolerable, condemns 'the remarriage of either during the lifetime of the first *for the very reason that it finally closes the door to all possibility of reconciliation and renewal of the broken vows* by involving one of the partners in new legal (and indeed moral) obligations which make return to the first partner virtually impossible'.[84] Our view is that it is not only remarriage which closes the door to all possibility of reconciliation and renewal. When that door has finally been shut by a determination of the will of either partner, there can be a freedom to remarry. But only if the door has been shut. Any children of the first marriage (almost invariably the chief casualties of divorce) are also of paramount importance, and the fulfilment of outstanding covenant obligations of parenthood towards them is another of the moral issues affecting the decision concerning remarriage.

A further important qualification needs to be made. Many marriages are broken because of some sort of personal inadequacy in maintaining faithfulness and upholding commitment. A good Christian marriage can provide one of the most fruitful contexts for the healing of personal immaturities and childhood hurts, but a bad marriage may only serve to deepen wounds and bring hurts exposed to the consciousness undealt with. To add the pain, guilt and tragedy of divorce to a stock of personal insecurity and need, is to make certain people very vulnerable indeed, and it is by no means a straightforward assumption that a second marriage will necessarily be any more successful than the first, unless such personal needs have been explored and some personal help received. A marriage failure should raise for some people the question of personal ability to make and sustain committed relationships; and the possibilities of therapy and Christian ministry on the one hand, and taking seriously a calling to future celibacy on the other, are further

moral issues to be weighed in the decision concerning remarriage.

Another qualification must be made before a person can be
said to be 'free' to remarry after divorce, and this is the moral
question of the social stability of marriage. It is not sufficient to
say that when a marriage has been irretrievably broken, the
couple are free to remarry. The social aspect of the marriage
covenant requires that we consider the overall stability of the
marriage and family pattern in society before that freedom is
asserted. R. A. McCormick comments helpfully:

> If divorce is a disvalue and if subsequent remarriage necessarily
> contains elements of disvalue (undermining of the stability of
> marriage) then it seems clear that one must have a proportionate
> reason for introducing this disvalue into the world. Under-
> emphasis on marriage as a social institution could lead one to
> overlook this dimension of the divorce-remarriage problem and
> conceive it one-sidedly in too personal terms.[85]

One would need to judge therefore that the overall personal
good of remarriage in a particular case would justify the threat
that a second union would make to the social institution of
marriage.

With these qualifications, and all other outstanding covenant
obligations to the first marriage fulfilled as far as possible, the
question concerning remarriage becomes: Is the promise of
sexual exclusiveness made in the first marriage covenant still
binding? It is difficult from the Scriptural recognition of remarriage after divorce to argue that it is. Certainly remarriage
falls under the shadow of previous failure, but even in those
New Testament passages which seem most clearly to speak of
remarriage as adultery (Mark 10:11f; Luke 16:18), we have
argued that the guilt of that sin lies in the initiatives taken to
break the first marriage (cf. Matt. 5:32). Both Testaments imply
that dissolution may be followed by subsequent marriage:
release from the person must also release from the vow. (There
are pastoral implications of this we shall need to refer to again.)

Having then agreed that freedom to remarry may be a real freedom for some people after divorce, there remains the question as to the appropriateness of the Church's blessing in any given case. This question, and the wider questions concerning the Church's responsibilities to divorced people generally, we explore in our final chapter.

SUMMARY OF CHAPTER 5

1 Divorce is 'covenant-breaking'. The marriage covenant is intended to be permanent and should not be broken. A covenant can in fact be broken, however, by an act of the will to abandon the commitment to the relationship. Such choice *can* destroy the covenant irreconcilably, though it does not necessarily do so. When it does then the question of civil divorce a rises.

2 A discussion of the relation between the teaching of Jesus and the Mosaic legislation leads to

3 Six principles:

(a) There should be no antithesis between an 'ethic of torah' and an 'ethic of disposition'.

(b) The Father's will for marriage has a general validity for all men.

(c) The Messiah's 'gift of righteousness' provides the possibility for the fulfilment of the Father's will that human marriage should be patterned on and display the character and meaning of God's covenant with his people.

(d) The teaching of Jesus is not to be interpreted merely as a new law code.

(e) The New Testament speaks both of the Father's will and also of his concessions made necessary because of sin.

(f) The 'Father's will' for marriage does not make unnecessary the sphere of civil legislation.

4 *Divorce* (a) Divorce is a moral act, not the result of 'misfortune'.

(b) To initiate civil divorce procedure as the 'lesser evil' may sometimes be a responsible choice, but only with the recognition of sin, with sorrow and repentance.

(c) The legal procedures of the 1969 legislation in this country do not seem to fulfil the intentions of the authors of the Anglican Report *Putting Asunder* (1966) on which (largely) they were based. The present legal situation and court procedures are in fact making divorce easier and the maintenance of marriage harder.

5 *Nullity*. Although some are urging the Church of England to follow the Church of Rome in exploring the possibilities of annulment in some cases of marital breakdown, it is sounder theologically and clearer in practice to recognize divorce, and to require the handling of even those 'marriages' which theologically may be deemed nullities to be the responsibility of civil courts.

6 *Remarriage*. After divorce, a person is legally and theologically 'free' to remarry, but such a course may not necessarily be wise (at least without counselling help), nor necessarily appropriate for the Church's blessing.

REFERENCES TO CHAPTER 5

1 Cf. O. M. T. O'Donovan, *Marriage and Permanence* (Grove, 1978), p. 17.
2 *Op. cit.*, p. 17f.
3 The original meaning of torah is instruction, and conveys the idea of divine teaching or revelation. It embraces much more than 'legislation' – it 'is the whole content of divine revelation "all that God has made known of His nature, character, purpose, and of what He would have man be and do"' (A. R. Vidler, *Christ's Strange Work*, quoting G. F. Moore, *Judaism*). Cf. also art. 'Law' in C. Brown (ed.), *Dictionary of New Testament Theology* Vol. 2. p. 440.
4 Cf. Matt. 7:21; many times in Matthew's Gospel Jesus refers to 'the Father's will' without further qualification; cf. 12:50, 18:14; 21:31, cf. Luke 12:47, 48.
5 Cf. H. Ridderbos, *The Coming of the Kingdom* (Presbyterian and Reformed, 1975), p. 296. Cf. here the doctrine of justification in the New Testament, and the relationship between justification and the 'active and passive' obedience of Christ: cf. T. F. Torrance, 'Justification: Its Radical Nature and Place in Reformed Doctrine and Life' in *Theology in Reconstruction* (SCM, 1965).
6 Compare refs in Chapter 3.
7 H. Ridderbos, *op. cit.*, p. 297ff of which the following sentences are a summary.
8 In one instance, Matt. 5:43, there is obvious conflict with O.T.
9 W. D. Davies, *The Setting of the Sermon on the Mount* (Cambridge, 1964), p. 104.
10 J. D. M. Derrett, *Law in the New Testament* (Darton, Longman

and Todd, 1970), p. 48f.

11 We do not need to repeat our discussion of the Pauline material from Chapter 4; the same emphases are discernible in the Epistles as in the Gospels.

12 Cf. H. Ridderbos, *op. cit.*, p. 306f.

13 *Ibid.*, p. 307.

14 Cf. R. E. Nixon, 'The Universality of the Concept of Law' in B. N. Kaye and G. J. Wenham (eds.), *Law, Morality and the Bible* (IVP, 1978), p. 62.

15 D. Field, *Taking Sides* (IVP, 1975), p. 75.

16 *Ibid.*

17 See Chapter 1.

18 H. Ridderbos, *op. cit.*, p. 258.

19 *Ibid.*, p. 247.

20 H. Oppenheimer, *The Marriage Bond* (The Faith Press, 1976), p. 60f.

21 Cf. H. Dooyeweerd, *A New Critique of Theoretical Thought* (Presbyterian and Reformed, ET 1969), p. 311f.

22 *Ibid.*

23 H. Thielicke, *The Ethics of Sex* (James Clarke, ET 1964), p. 164.

24 *Ibid.*, p. 165.

25 C. E. B. Cranfield, *St Mark* (Cambridge, 1959; revised 1966), p. 320.

26 H. Ridderbos, *op. cit.*, p. 308.

27 *Ibid.*

28 *Ibid.*, p. 309.

29 Thus J. Calvin, *Institutes of the Christian Religion* II. vii. 6-14:

> The 'moral law' . . . consists of three parts.
>
> The first part is this: while it shows God's righteousness, that is the righteousness alone acceptable to God, it warns, informs, convicts, and lastly condemns, every man of his own unrighteousness . . .
>
> The second function of the law is this: at least by fear of punishment to restrain certain men who are untouched by any care for what is just and right unless compelled by hearing the dire threats in the law . . .
>
> The third and principal use which pertains more closely to the proper purpose of the law, finds its place among believers in whose hearts the Spirit of God already lives and reigns.

Cf. H. Bullinger in the eighth Sermon of the Third *Decade*, Parker Society edition (1850), iii, pp. 236-45.

The order of exposition is different in Vidler and Calvin.

30 A. R. Vidler, *Christ's Strange Work* (Longmans, 1944), p. 27.

31 *Ibid.*, p. 38.

32 *Ibid.*, p. 52.

33 *Ibid.*, p. 27.

34 Cf. William Temple's comments: 'To say that you cannot make folk good by Act of Parliament is to utter a dangerous half-truth. You cannot by Act of Parliament make men morally good; but you can by Act of Parliament supply conditions which facilitate the growth of moral goodness and remove conditions which obstruct it.' Quoted in Kaye and Wenham, *op. cit.*, p. 244.

35 *Marriage, Divorce and the Church* (SPCK, 1972), p. 123.

36 *Ibid.*, p. 71.

37 *Ibid.*, p. 121.

38 D. Field, *op. cit.*, p. 76.

39 Cf. Chapter 1 ref. 29.

40 J. Murray, *Divorce*, (Presbyterian and Reformed, 1961), p. 90f.

41 The whole chapter 'Why get married?' in L. Smedes's altogether excellent book *Sex for Christians* is of interest here.

42 D. O'Callaghan, 'Theology and Divorce', *Irish Theological Quarterly, 37* (1970), p. 218f.

43 Cf. e.g. the discussion of Rom. 13:1ff in O. Cullmann, *The State in the New Testament* (SCM, 1957), p. 56f and C. Brown (ed.), *Dictionary of New Testament Theology* Vol. 3 (1978), p. 97.

44 D. O'Callaghan, *op. cit.*, p. 214.

45 *Ibid.*, p. 222.

46 L. Smedes, *The Reformed Journal*, October 1976, p. 10.

47 J. Murray, *op. cit.*, p. 96f.

48 P. Ramsey, *Basic Christian Ethics* (Scribners, 1950), p. 71.

49 *Ibid.*, p. 72.

50 Cf. O. M. T. O'Donovan, 'Marriage and the Family' in J. R. W. Stott (ed.), *Obeying Christ in a Changing World* (Fount, 1977) Vol. 3. p. 108.

51 *Op. cit.*

52 Cf. here K. Barth, *Church Dogmatics, 3/4*, p. 212.

53 Matrimonial Causes Act 1973 (in which the Divorce Reform Act 1969 is consolidated with other legislation).

54 Cf. discussion in Chapter 1 and Chapter 6.

55 H. Oppenheimer, *op. cit.*, p. 75.

56 viz. adultery, unreasonable behaviour, desertion, separation.

57 His Honour Judge Irvine, 'Present Trends in Divorce Law' in

The Theology and Meaning of Marriage (CLA, 1978), p. 14.
58 *Ibid.*, p. 15.
59 *Ibid.*
60 *Ibid.*
61 *Ibid.*, p. 16.
62 Cheslyn Jones (ed.), *For Better, For Worse* (CLA, 1977)[2], p. 55.
(Since this chapter was completed, the Family Law Sub-Committee of the Contentious Business Committee of the Law Society's Council, has published a discussion paper on the Reform of the Divorce Law, and the setting up of a Family Court: *A Better Way Out* (1979), discussed in the Law Society's *Gazette* on 14 March 1979. Their primary recommendations are twofold. First, the only ground for divorce should be the irretrievable breakdown of marriage as shown by one year's separation between the spouses immediately prior to petition. Secondly, a family court should be set up with exclusive jurisdiction in all family matters (divorce, custody, maintenance, etc.); its procedure should be of an inquisitorial rather than adversarial nature, and a welfare and counselling service to give advice and help people to adjust to breakdown aftermath, should be attached to it.

The intention behind the first proposal is to remove the remaining traces in the existing law of 'the concept of divorce as a contest', and – recognizing that only a minority of petitions are disputed, seeks to make the process of ending a marriage as smooth and pain-free as possible. If this proposal is accepted, however, it will remove any remaining notion of offence (and responsibility?) from the law regulating divorce, it will remove any suggestion that the law serves a normative function in restricting easy divorce and thereby strengthening the possibilities for marriage, and it may well encourage divorce as the first option in marital pain among many who could have found the way of reconciliation had the barriers to easy divorce been firmer.

The second proposal for a family court, associated with a counselling service, is intended to make the court facilities more accessible to those in need, and to promote a more informal approach to the problems of deciding on custody, maintenance, and so on. Clearly this will be tidier than the present system, will ease some of the tension once the decision to divorce has been taken, and will provide needed help in conciliation through counselling. It is unfortunate, however, that all concern for reconciliation before divorce (still hinted at in the present law) seems now to disappear. The proposal would, it seems, finally remove the judicial function from the decision concerning divorce as such, and leave the entire decision about the ending of a marriage to the partners themselves.

There is no space for adequate treatment of all that these proposals entail. It would seem that, in the light of our earlier discussion, there are some large question marks to be placed over both of them.)

63 Cf. A. R. Winnett, *Divorce and Remarriage in Anglicanism* (Macmillan, 1958), p. 4f.

64 R. Brown, *Marriage Annulment in the Catholic Church* (Kevin Mayhew, 1977), p. 5.

65 M. Puxon, *Family Law* (Penguin, 1963, 1971), p. 107ff.

66 *Ibid.*, p. 22 quoting Corbett v. Corbett (1970).

67 *Ibid.*, p. 115f.

68 C. M. Chavasse, 'Nullity', *The Churchman*, Dec. 1965, p. 192; cf. *The Church and the Law of Nullity of Marriage* (SPCK, 1955), p. 48.

69 Puxon, *op. cit.*, p. 120.

70 *Ibid.*, p. 121. Puxon quotes Sir Francis Jeune's Judgement of 1897:

> No fraudulent concealment or misrepresentation enables the defrauded party who has consented to it (the marriage) to rescind it . . . There must be the voluntary consent of both parties . . . but when in English law fraud is spoken of as a ground of avoiding a marriage, this does not include a consent, but is limited to such fraud as procures the appearance without the reality of consent.

71 R. Brown, *op. cit.*, p. 9f.

72 *Ibid.*, p. 5f.

73 W. M. Abbott, *The Documents of Vatican II*, p. 250f.

74 R. Brown, *op. cit.*, cf. discussion in *African Christian Marriage* (1977), p. 50f.

75 e.g. Archbishop Zoghbi at the fourth session of Vatican II, quoted in D. O'Callaghan, *op. cit.*, p. 210.

76 Chavasse, *op. cit.*, p. 192.

77 K. E. Kirk, *Marriage and Divorce* (Hodder, 1948), p. 67.

78 *Op. cit.*, p. 50.

79 J. Dominian, 'Marital Breakdown', *The Ampleforth Journal*,

LXXXIII pt. 1 (1968), and in *Marriage, Divorce and the Church*, p. 148.

80 *Marriage, Divorce and the Church*, p. 149.

81 There are biblical instances of vows which though lightly made are still binding in e.g. Num. 30:6f; Prov. 20:25; Eccles. 5:1ff.

82 Chavasse, *op. cit.*, p. 193 quoting Lord Stowell, (1811).

83 H. Thielicke, *op. cit.*, p. 169.

84 K. E. Kirk. *op. cit.*, p. 86.

85 R. A. McCormick S.J., 'Notes on Moral Theology: (3) Divorce and Remarriage', *Theological Studies*, 36 (1975), p. 100f, esp. p. 115.

CHAPTER 6

Divorce and Remarriage

The Pastoral Problems

1. Building for Faithfulness

I do not believe that people in the throes of marital agony will listen to the repetition of a moral rule against divorce unless their characters have much earlier disposed them toward accepting permanence and working toward a reasonably constructive relationship within the permanent structure.[1]

Once again L. Smedes is right in focusing the central pastoral point in the problems of marriage breakdown.

It has been said that the Church of England has become 'obsessed with divorce', and certainly a reading of the Convocation debates of 1937-8 and the Synod debates following the Root Report of 1971 and the Lichfield Report of 1978 would indicate that many churchmen in the Church of England believe that the proper way to strengthen and uphold the Christian view of marriage can be reduced to making divorce as difficult as possible, and to regarding remarriage after divorce as in every case inappropriate for the Church's blessing.

However, as we sought to show in Chapter 1, though always contrary to God's will for marriage, divorce is often a symptom of a far deeper problem in contemporary society – for Christians as for others – than simply the personal failure of a particular couple within their marriage relationship. This is not to say that marriage breakdown is not the responsibility of the partners to the marriage: breakdown is the result of the actions of their wills and the choices they have made. It is to say, however, that the structure and expectations of contemporary society make the exercise of those choices increasingly more difficult for some people. We quoted J. Richard Udry's comment that 'the kind of marriage Americans believe in simply has high divorce rates'.[2] He argues that the high rates of divorce correspond to the prevailing cultural expectations about marriage and to the fact that divorce is much less socially stigmatized than before. These facts are both associated with the rapid social upheavals of recent decades, and as we noted in Chapter 1, many trends in contemporary society do not promote marital stability, rather the reverse. Udry himself comments that the only course of action which is likely significantly to lower the divorce rate is a return to 'a rural, religious, non-industrialized way of life which is compatible with families as economic production units'. 'Nothing short of this is likely to restore the marital stability of 1870. Courts of reconciliation, waiting periods, highschool and marriage courses – all of these things may help some, but none will help much. The kind of marriage Americans believe in simply has high divorce rates.'[3]

Commenting on Udry's assessment, Hebden Taylor argues that the problem of divorce will not be solved legally, 'but only by changing the contemporary climate of opinion regarding the nature and purpose of marriage'.

> Our generation is now faced with the necessity of choosing the gods it wishes to serve, and it must realize what fateful moral, social and *marital* consequences hang upon that choice. Life is religion, not morality nor the pursuit of one's selfish happiness. Life is religion, and involves the service of the one true God whom Jesus Christ has revealed or of a false god and idol of man's own devising. For this reason Christians must work first to bring about a religious change in the direction of men's lives and hearts before they can hope to persuade them to adopt Christian standards regarding the sanctity of marriage ties.[4]

This goes part of the way towards an answer. It points up the fact that simply to concentrate on more stringent divorce legislation is not the most important Christian response (important as changes in the legal procedures may well be). It focuses the problem of divorce in the understanding of marriage. But it does not give a full enough answer. A change back to 1870, to pre-industrial rural religious family life, is not a live option for most people. And it is not only those without Christian faith who are suffering the pain of marital breakdown: Christians too, despite their affirmation of God's will for the permanence of marriage, can find themselves in situations (for which they share responsibility) in which divorce can seem the only responsible choice.

The pastoral problem for the Church, as L. Smedes indicated in the quotation at the heading of this chapter, is how to foster and encourage the personal qualities which make for covenant-faithfulness and commitment, even within the pressures of contemporary society. How do people become disposed towards fidelity? How can the Church help them to stand against the disintegrating forces of modern living? How can the Church help people to be loyal to each other, to live for each other as well as for themselves, to accept the commitment to permanence and maintain a relationship of trust, acceptance, forbearance and forgiveness? And how can the Church exercise its ministry towards the wider society, with a view to minimizing its anti-marriage pressures and forces of disintegration?

As Dr Dominian has argued, modern marriage, with its rediscovery of the internal meaning of covenant-love relationships, which has always been at the heart of the Christian understanding of marriage, despite its obscurity in much ecclesiastical preoccupation with externals, can be just the context in which substantial personal growth and fulfilment can be achieved.[5] How can the Church assist this achievement to become a reality rather than, as so often, a seemingly unattainable dream? These are the pastoral problems to which the Church must address itself.

The question of the age at which people marry is not unimportant. Dr Dominian comments that 'every study seems to confirm that age at marriage is important for ultimate stability. Those under twenty are specially vulnerable.'[6] He argues that a great deal of preventative work can begin through 'the art of persuasion': while granting that people must be free to marry if they wish, it can be a pastoral duty to persuade against early marriage. Particularly when the social pressures to legitimize a child are the primary reason for hasty marriage, pastoral advice may sometimes have to be that 'marriage is not the answer'.[7] It is arguable that the Church of England ought to take this more seriously still, and explore the wisdom of insisting on a minimum age for church marriage. It was reported in *The Tablet* of 29 April 1978 that the Bishop of the Roman Catholic Diocese of Hull, Quebec, has declared that no one under eighteen may be married in a church in his diocese. This policy – probably unique in the Roman Catholic world – is a direct response to the increasing number of divorces and separations particularly among the young. It is a policy the Church of England would also do well to think about carefully. But it could not do so without also thinking about the social deprivation which some-times forces early marriage.

Proposals such as Dr Dominian's Institute for the Family,[8] as a research and servicing agency within the Church, and the programmes of Education for Marriage suggested in the Report of the Church Union Commission's *The Theology and Meaning of Marriage*[9] also need, despite Udry's caveats, to be explored. As Michael Pollitt rightly comments: 'Education for and within marriage is a much more urgent matter than the question of the remarriage of divorced people.'[10] It is good that some agencies are growing, and pamphlets like 'Preparation for Marriage' published by Care and Counsel are being used in parishes.[11] But much more could be done. There is much to be said for the development of required courses in marriage preparation (at least as significant as confirmation preparation!), preferably at Deanery level, to which all prospective church-marriage couples could be referred, and be asked to attend as part of the preliminaries to a church wedding. In time it could become a standard procedure. It might well result in a reduction in the number of church weddings; it might, however, lead to an increase in stable marriages which do actually serve as a witness to the world of what God intends marriage to be.

At the very least, General and Diocesan Synods should seek to promote every aid towards more adequate marriage preparation, to develop and make available counselling skills, and promote the kind of education which will help foster characters which are more able to enter and sustain relationships of covenanted faithfulness, relationships which are themselves healing and growth environments and which in fact prove to be indissoluble.

In one sense, of course, preparation for marriage begins at birth; the whole of the Church's parochial ministry to a person and a family (at Sunday School age and before) can contribute towards fostering the growth of such character.

Agencies of Reconciliation

The 1969 divorce legislation requires the solicitor to certify whether he has discussed the question of reconciliation with the petitioner, before court proceedings begin.[12] While this is right and proper, as we noted, this has tended to become mere formality, and is not itself instrumental in furthering reconciliation, largely because by the time the matter has reached the solicitor, it is usually too late to broach the question of reconciliation.

This is not to say, however, that the provision of agencies to aid reconciliation is not necessary. On the contrary they are essential, and it is by no means sufficient for the Church to abdicate its responsibilities in this field to secular counselling agencies. As the Church plays a prominent place in the ceremonies by which many marriages are made, so the Church is necessarily involved in the pain and tragedy if such marriages break down.

Canon A. P. Shepherd has argued[13] that it should be the

duty of those married in church to seek the help of the Church at the first threat of any breakdown in their marriage. It is certainly arguable that at the least those ostensibly affirming their acceptance of the Christian view of marriage by asking for the Church's blessing at their wedding, should be strongly encouraged – if their affirmation is to be taken seriously – to seek the help and support of their Church if the marriage reaches serious difficulties. And it is the duty of the Church to be an agency of reconciliation in such circumstances.

By such a procedure, Shepherd argues, many a church marriage might well be saved from ever reaching the divorce court.

But how can such a procedure be encouraged? At the end of the prolonged debates on marriage in the Lower House of Convocation in Canterbury in 1937, the then Archdeacon of Dudley proposed:

> That an instruction be added to the Marriage Service to be read by the priest to the newly-married, to the effect that they had by their marriage in church publicly accepted the Christian standard of marriage, and that if circumstances threatened to break the true marital relationship between them, it would be their duty to consult their parish priest or bishop before having recourse to legal action.[14]

In the event he agreed to withdraw the motion, largely because the question of amendment to the Book of Common Prayer was a separate large issue, and the main concern of Convocation at that time was pastoral discipline. Nevertheless the proposal received a sympathetic hearing, but no action was taken.

Essentially the same point was intended in the final part of the Act of Convocation declared as such by Archbishop Fisher in 1957:

> Recognizing that pastoral care may well avert the danger of divorce if it comes into play before legal proceedings have been started, this House urges all clergy in their preparation of couples for marriage to tell them, both for their own sakes and for that of

their friends, that the good offices of the clergy are always available.[15]

It is doubtful whether such a recommendation could be sufficient to establish such consultation as a regular procedure. There is little evidence to suggest that it has. Canon Shepherd himself proposed an exhortation in the Marriage Service which urged that:

> It is incumbent on those who are married, if at any time circumstances should arise which appear to them to threaten the stability of their marriage, that as soon as possible and before any other action is taken, they should seek counsel and advice on the matter from their parish priest or the bishop or someone appointed by him.[16]

Whether such a change in the Marriage Service itself is the right procedure may be open to question. What is unambiguously clear, however, is the God-given role the Church must seek to re-establish for itself as a ministry of reconciliation in situations of personal enmity. Is the need for Diocesan Marriage Counselling Services? Or for more training for ordinands and clergy in the skills of marriage counselling? Does each parish or group of parishes need to select and equip some married couples as counsellors?

Whatever the practical steps needed, the Church has a duty to make itself known, and inspire confidence in its value, as the agency within which the reconciling grace of God can become a reality in the strained relationships of marriage breakdown. And it must work towards establishing as a regular procedure, the use of that agency as a first resort by married couples at times of marital distress.

It is to the Church's shame that there sometimes seems to be more help available in secular counselling agencies than in the Body of Christ.

2. When Marriages are Broken

The pastoral questions for the Church when a marriage has

broken beyond all reasonable hope of repair are twofold. On the one hand, there is the question of *acceptance*. For too long the primary stance of the Church to people who have been divorced has been one of condemnation or rejection. This is not to say that Church discipline is unimportant. Nor is it to say that the Church does not have a proclamatory role in making clear God's opposition to divorce alongside his will for marriage. But the Christian community is called also to display that character of God which is seen in the acceptance of sinners as persons whatever their failure, and in helping them towards finding God's restoring grace. The Christian community needs to learn how to express compassion towards the divorced person 'as victim'. 'Naturally divorced persons are never merely victims . . . but most these days are victims of divorce as well as agents who decided on divorce.'[17] And just as contemporary society tends to increase the pressures and frustrations in fractured relationships and tends to decrease support for relationships of permanent commitment, so when divorce occurs, the patterns and expectancies of our society can magnify the sense of isolation, shame, failure and accusing guilt. 'The Christian community fails miserably in its calling to be a redemptive community if it has no feeling for the divorced person as victim.'[18]

The Lambeth Fathers in 1948 expressed a similar concern for the 'special pastoral duty and responsibility' the Church needs to exercise towards divorced persons 'whether they are sinners whose wilfulness or misconduct has wrecked their marriage, or casualties of marriages entered upon "unadvisedly, lightly or wantonly" as is so often in wartime, or the victims of abominable treatment or desertion'.[19] Part of the pastoral question for the Church is to ask how best it can be an agency of support and acceptance to the victims of divorce.

And the second pastoral question is how best the Church can aid the divorced person, and his or her family, in finding 'the Father's will' for their future. The pastor may well be needed in unravelling the questions of real guilt and the need for forgiveness from God from (sometimes false) psychological guilt feelings arising from the sense of failure and personal tragedy. Assistance in confession of sin and receiving God's forgiveness can often be of very great importance. As Cruse and Green commented, forgiveness is also due to the other partner: 'There should always be pardon for the other partner, even if restored fellowship is impossible.' There may well need to be pastoral advice on how to discharge any outstanding covenant obligations remaining from the marriage. For some, but surely not all, the covenanted obligation of sexual exclusiveness may lead them to view their future life as divorcee as a calling to celibacy. The covenant obligations extend to providing love and emotional and physical security for children. The divorced parent needs help and support and maybe practical assistance in seeking to maximize the fulfilment of that obligation as far as possible. There are, of course, innumerable other needs, sometimes financial, always emotional and spiritual, which crowd on to the divorced person. The needs vary from situation to situation. The Christian community itself is called to be a healing and supportive environment in which some, at least, of these needs can be met, and others worked through and gradually coped with.

The Question of Remarriage

We have (Chapter 5) argued that a divorced person is no longer married to his/her former partner, and that there are certain circumstances in which he/she may in conscience believe it right to marry again, and be morally free to do so. It is part of the pastoral task of the Church to assist such a person in their questions of conscience and of continuing obligations and also, as we have said, in the prior questions of penitence and restitution which must be dealt with before the issue of remarriage is even raised.

It is to such circumstances that the following paragraphs are addressed. The moral question of the propriety of repeating lifelong vows is not as central as some argue. John Lucas in

For Better, For Worse, for example, says that 'a solemn vow once made and broken continues to be of moral relevance . . . If I have made a solemn vow and not kept it, I may well be forgiven, but can hardly be sincere in my penitence if I think myself free to make a new, though different, one all over again.'[20] On this, however, two comments may be made. First, we quoted Helen Oppenheimer's view that the vow is a vow to a *person*: it is a promise to *marry*, and, as O'Donovan puts it, when the marriage is irretrievably destroyed (and even for some Christians that may be true), 'there can be no distinct obligation to respect the vows apart from respecting the marriage'.[21] Secondly, while – to be sure – any failure reduces one's moral credibility for the next time, if that was all that could be said, all our sins would accumulate against us. It is not clear why it is thought impossible to be sincere in penitence for the past, and at the same time hope for a new start in the future. Indeed, sometimes it is the recognition of the mistake, indeed sin, in making the first vows which is being expressed in the penitence for divorce. And as Cruse and Green commented from their pastoral experience: 'It is quite untrue to say that a person who has broken a lifelong vow cannot make another. Practical experience demonstrates that when there has been repentance, the new vows can be made with utter sincerity.'[22]

Whereas, therefore, the moral question concerning the right of remarriage may be fairly clear, the pastoral question as to the Church's role in such remarriage, in particular whether or not it should give its blessing to any particular remarriage, is much more complex. The Church has other needs to consider than only those of the couple concerned; it is here that the tension between the Church's prophetic and pastoral callings can be most acute. It needs to give institutional expression both to the Father's will for the permanence of marriage, and to the Gospel of forgiveness for the penitent.

Focusing first on the couple requesting marriage after one or both of them have been divorced, the pastoral problems concern the difficulty of translating the proper theological distinctions (those who would not, from those who could not, keep covenant), into workable pastoral categories, without recourse to a legalistic casuistry. The theological distinctions between 'guilt' and 'innocence' are rarely if ever fully clear-cut in a marriage breakdown, and although some 'offences' (desertion, physical adultery) are clearly definable, others which are equally destructive of a marriage (mental cruelty, unfaithfulness of attitude) are not.

The practice of refusing to marry *any* divorced person with the Church's blessing seems unfortunately to witness only to the fact that Church law must always come before personal need. And yet, of course, indiscriminate remarriage on demand would seem to speak of a God of cheap grace who is blind to sin. If the Church is to give its blessing to some who seek remarriage after divorce, it needs first to be sure that it is pastorally possible to operate a consistent, fair and adequate discrimination. What are the criteria for such discrimination? Criteria based on past guilt or innocence are difficult to operate pastorally, and if penitence for sin has been real, to determine the future by the (now forgiven) sin of the past, seems to suggest that matrimonial offences are among the sins which are unforgivable. The only feasible criteria on which the Church can decide whether or not it is appropriate to give its blessing concern not degrees of guilt, but present attitude. In exploring such attitudes in pastoral interview there would need to be concern for real penitence for the past, including the present attitude to the former spouse, and the sort of commitment intended for the new marriage. Sometimes it is the very pain of a previous breakdown that results in the conversion of the person to Christ, and an experience of his forgiving grace.

The Church's blessing for any marriage should be reserved only for those who share its view of marriage, and the condition (with respect to the couple) on which the Church's blessing on second marriage should be decided, is penitence for past sin and a genuine desire to seek God's grace for a new marriage which accords with his pattern.

It is when we focus, secondly, on the question of *how* the Church's blessing can be given without at the same time cheapening its witness to God's will for marriage, that the difficulties multiply. There seem to be three main options.

(a) Pastoral Interview followed by full Marriage Service in church

The majority proposal of the Lichfield Report of 1978 was that in certain cases divorced persons might be admitted to be married in church following a pastoral enquiry. The Report rightly noted that 'for any scheme of selective remarriage to work, it must be clear that the occasions when remarriage in church occur are exceptional and determined by a consistent policy'.[23] The signatories then argue that the only way to ensure that this happens is to require the decision in each case to be taken by the bishop or by members of a small panel nominated by the bishop to act on his behalf. At this point the Lichfield Report differed from the Root Commission, which considered that the responsibility for the decision should rest in each case with the parish priest concerned.[24] However, the reasoning by which it would seem invidious to lay the whole responsibility on the shoulders of the parish priest[25] would seem to apply *mutatis mutandis* to a diocesan panel. As the minority of the Lichfield Commission themselves argue convincingly, 'the attempt to operate the procedure . . . in a pastoral manner would make it impossible to maintain effective standards and to secure a consistent approach throughout the dioceses. It would soon appear that some dioceses were following a harder and some a softer line, and the practice of a diocese might well change with a change of bishop.'[26] Consistency, they argue, could only be achieved by a sort of juridical approach 'founded on case-law and precedent'; this would most likely lead to a tendency to avoid hard cases and relax standards, and lead in the end to indiscriminate remarriage.

(b) Pastoral Interview followed by a Service of Blessing

In their pamphlet of 1949, Cruse and Green urged the official sanctioning of Services of Blessing which many clergy were using for couples following civil marriage.[27] They believed that the refusal of the actual marriage in church was the best way to operate a consistent discipline which witnessed to the fact that divorce was at best the lesser evil, but that the welcome to a service in church subsequent to the civil marriage could demonstrate in appropriate cases that the Church was glad to give its blessing. Bishop Kirk had criticized the practice severely in his book *Marriage and Divorce*.[28] The Resolution (to which Bishop Kirk refers), promulgated as Act of Convocation in 1957, reads

> No public service shall be held for those who have contracted a civil marriage after divorce. It is not within the competence of the Convocations to lay down what private prayers the curate in the exercise of his pastoral ministry may say with the persons concerned, or to issue regulations as to where or when these prayers shall be said.[29]

It was therefore the intention of the Convocation ruling to forbid what is becoming increasingly prevalent (often with episcopal approval): a public service in church with full publicity, and everything done in church as far as possible like a conventional wedding service, except the actual vows. Bishop Kirk's comment is that 'I would far rather that they flouted the Resolution altogether, and boldly used the Prayer Book in such cases, than that they should evolve such sham marriages out of their own imaginings, hoping that the result will appear almost as good as the real thing. Less harm would be done this way than the other; for at least everyone would know that what was involved was a genuine and far-reaching clash of conviction and not a disloyal underground movement . . .'[30] The Lichfield Report likewise unanimously recommended that such services be abandoned, on the grounds that the confusion between such services and the Marriage Service itself did not aid the Church in any of its witness.[31]

The primary point at issue here, though, is not so much one of confusion caused to onlookers, as confusion in the Church's own position. Is the Church in a particular case glad to give its blessing to the marriage of a divorced person or not? If the answer is no, the Service of Blessing should not be given (but on what grounds can it be refused?); if the answer is yes, it is not clear what is gained by denying the priest his role as registrar, while retaining his role as the one who gives the Church's blessing. This practice if officially sanctioned would lead to services of blessing on demand, because it would be considerably more difficult to withhold a blessing service if asked for it, than it would to refuse the full Marriage Service; unlike the Marriage Service itself, no commitment is expressed.

(c) Pastoral preparation followed by a special Marriage Service

Assuming that after pastoral consultation, the parish priest and the couple believe in conscience that it is appropriate to have a church service for their marriage – and, to aid the priest in his decision, a diocesan panel may well be a helpful advisory aid – it would appear that neither the Marriage Service as it stands, nor a Service of Blessing following civil marriage, gives adequate witness to the view that God's will for marriage is for permanence, that divorce is sin, but that sin can be forgiven. The most satisfactory option appears to be a procedure which combines adequate pastoral preparation with a liturgical service which itself gives appropriate witness to the Church's prophetic and pastoral roles. A form of service is needed, in which the marriage itself is included, which can act in a discriminatory way by expressing both God's will for marriage and penitence for the sin of divorce. If both such facts are publicly declared in the liturgy itself, the important distinctions in the Church's witness between first and second marriages can be maintained. What is envisaged is specifically a 'Service of Holy Matrimony to be used when one or both parties have been divorced'. There would need to be an introduction declaring the Christian doctrine of marriage, noting that one or both partners had been divorced, and that they had in pastoral consultation expressed penitence for any sin in the breakdown of the previous marriage, and a genuine desire to seek the help and grace of God to keep the vows which were about to be made. Such an introduction would appropriately be followed by a call to share in a public act of penitence by both couple and congregation. The inclusion of such an act in the service would draw attention to the shadow under which all marriages involving a divorced person fall. It could hardly be appropriate for such confession to be made only by the divorced person: the general confession might be too general, and a specific confession belongs to private and not to public worship. Helmut Thielicke also comments, in a slightly different context:

> Announcements with comments made in church concerning specific cases of this kind and using them to make reference to the essential indissolubility of marriage are undoubtedly impossible in a national Church. For it is more than questionable whether the condition of our congregations would permit us to presuppose the kind of mature spiritual understanding which would be necessary here in order not actually to provoke Pharisaic pride.[32]

But a public act of penitence in which couple and congregation *both* join could be used to show (indeed the call to penitence should specify) that the sin of a broken marriage is the responsibility both of the partners to the former marriage, and also of the whole society which sometimes places burdens upon marriage which are too great to bear. Couple and congregation together would join in confession for the sins which cause and contribute to divorce. Then would follow the full Marriage Service. The Lichfield Commission rightly urged against any change of wording in the vows: 'Those coming to the Church to be remarried after divorce would need to be reminded as clearly as possible that the commitment they entered into was identical with that they undertook in the first marriage'.[33]

Such a substantial modification of the Marriage Service, while retaining the same vows, could be framed itself to act in a discriminatory way. Those who in pastoral preparation believed in conscience that they could take part in such a service should be welcomed on the basis of their word. But very careful preparation would need to be given, so that as far as possible those who took part in such a service understood that the responsibility before God for doing so rested with them.

It would be very appropriate to make the Holy Communion a normal part of such a service. In that those who are married in this way will be those only who have expressed penitence for sin and the desire by God's grace to live in his will for the future, the welcome to Holy Communion will be appropriate for them, and its use encouraged, for this is the service by which most effectively the dual witness to God's law and God's grace is made. As Michael Ward notes: 'By this means, the people and the ceremony are placed plainly under the Lord Jesus Christ, and the Church's witness is not so much to its own role as to him as Lord and Saviour.'[34]

SUMMARY OF CHAPTER 6

1 A primary task in marriage preparation is the enabling of the growth of characters capable of faithfulness and loving commitment.
2 The Church must seek to re-establish its role as an agency of reconciliation; and by teaching and pastoral practice in situations of marital pain proclaim the Gospel of grace, forgiveness, and restoration.
3 When marriages are broken, the Church's concern includes acceptance, support and help for those in pain, and enabling those concerned in discovering the will of God for their future.
4 The most appropriate response for remarriage which holds together the Church's prophetic and pastoral responsibilities, would seem to be the availability of a service distinct from the normal Marriage Service, including a note of penitence for past sin as well as the vows of the new marriage and the hopes and prayers for the joy of the future. Such a service if used with adequate pastoral pre-

paration could itself act in a discriminatory way in the decision concerning the rightness of the Church's blessing in a particular case.

REFERENCES TO CHAPTER 6

1 L. Smedes, *The Reformed Journal*, October 1976, p. 12.
2 Quoted in E. L. Hebden Taylor, *The Reformational Understanding of Family and Marriage* (1970), p. 31; cf. Ch. 1 ref. 22.
3 *Ibid*.
4 Hebden Taylor, *op. cit.*, p. 31f.
5 Cf. e.g. *Cycles of Affirmation* (Darton, Longman and Todd, 1975), p. 61ff.
6 *The Clergy Review*, Dec. 1973, p. 931.
7 *Ibid.*, p. 932.
8 Appended note to Appendix 6 in *Marriage, Divorce and the Church* (1971), p. 150.
9 p. 22ff.
10 *Ibid*.
11 'Preparation for Marriage' by Myra Chave Jones and Sarah Howarth, published by CARE AND COUNSEL, 146 Queen Victoria Street, London, EC4V 4BX, from which copies are obtainable by post.
12 See our discussion, Chapter 5, above.
13 A. P. Shepherd, *Marriage Was Made for Man* (Methuen, 1958).
14 *The Chronicle of Convocation* (May 1937) No. 2, p. 442.
15 *The Chronicle of Convocation* (1957) No. 2, p. 205f.
16 Shepherd, *op. cit.*
17 L. Smedes, *op. cit.*, p. 13.
18 *Ibid*.
19 *Report of the Lambeth Conference* 1948, p. 98.
20 J. Lucas, *Frustrated Vows?* in *For Better, For Worse* (1977)[2], p. 37.
21 O. O'Donovan, 'Marriage and the Family' in J. R. W. Stott (ed.), *Obeying Christ in a Changing World*, vol. 3 (1977), p. 108.
22 J. H. Cruse and B. S. W. Green, *Marriage, Divorce and Repentance in the Church of England* (Hodder, 1949).
23 *Marriage and the Church's Task* (CIO, 1978), p. 85.
24 *Ibid*.
25 *Ibid*.
26 *Ibid.*, p. 94f.

27 Cruse and Green, *op. cit.*
28 K. E. Kirk, *Marriage and Divorce* (Hodder, 1948)², p. 135.
29 Cf. ref. 15 above.
30 Kirk, *op. cit.*, p. 135.
31 *Marriage and the Church's Task*, p. 84.
32 H. Thielicke, *The Ethics of Sex* (James Clarke, 1964), p. 189.
33 *Marriage and the Church's Task*, p. 86.
34 M. Ward, 'Once Married Always Married?' – Issues for further study; an unpublished continuation of Mr Ward's earlier paper in *The Churchman*, Vol. 87/3 (Autumn 1973), p. 190.

Bibliography

W. Abbott S.J. (ed.), *The Documents of Vatican II* (G. Chapman, 1966).

F. Alwyn Adams, *Divorce* (1949).

J. P. V. Balsdon, *Roman Women* (Bodley Head, 1962).

D. Sherwin Bailey, *The Man-Woman Relation in Christian Thought* (SCM, 1959).

The Mystery of Love and Marriage (SCM, 1952).

R. Banks, *Jesus and the Law in the Synoptic Tradition* (Cambridge, 1975).

C. K. Barrett, *A Commentary on the First Epistle to the Corinthians* (A. & C. Black, 1971)[2].

K. Barth, *Church Dogmatics*, 3/4 (T. & T. Clark, ET 1961).

F. W. Beare, *The Earliest Records of Jesus* (Blackwell, 1962).

Becon's Works, Parker Society edition.

G. C. Berkouwer, *Man: The Image of God* (Eerdmans, 1962).

J. Bernard, *The Future of Marriage* (Penguin, 1972).

L. Boettner, *Divorce* (Presbyterian and Reformed, 1960).

A. H. Box and C. Gore, *Divorce in the New Testament* (SPCK, 1921).

C. Brown (ed.), *The New International Dictionary of New Testament Theology* (Paternoster, Vol. 1, 1975; Vol. 2, 1976; Vol. 3, 1978).

F. Brown, 'Divorce and Remarriage: Is the Church of England Right?', *Faith and Worship* (Winter 1977-8), p. 3.

R. Brown, *Marriage Annulment in the Catholic Church* (Kevin Mayhew, 1977).

M. Bucer, *De Regno Christi*.

Bullinger's Decades, Parker Society edition.

J. Calvin, *Commentary on a Harmony of the Evangelists*.

D. R. Catchpole, 'The Synoptic Divorce Material as a Traditio-Historical Problem', Bulletin of John Rylands' University Library of Manchester, 57, No. 1 (1974).

R. H. Charles, *The Teaching of the New Testament on Divorce* (William and Norgate, 1921).

F. H. Chase, *What did Christ teach about Divorce?* (1921).

Concilium Vol. 5. No. 6 (1970), 'The Future of Marriage as an Institution'.

C. E. B. Cranfield, *St Mark* (Cambridge, 1966).

T. Cranmer, 'A Confutation of Unwritten Verities' in *Works* Vol. 2.

H. Crouzel, 'Remarriage after Divorce in the Primitive Church', *Irish Theological Quarterly, 38* (1971), p. 21.

J. H. Cruse and B. S. W. Green, *Marriage, Divorce and Repentance in the Church of England* (Hodder, 1949).

C. E. Curran, *Catholic Moral Theology in Dialogue* (Fides Publishers, 1972).

W. D. Davies, *The Setting of the Sermon on the Mount* (Cambridge, 1964).

J. D. M. Derrett, *Law in the New Testament* (Darton, Longman and Todd, 1970).

R. De Vaux, *Ancient Israel* (McGraw Hill Co., 1965).

A. G. Dickens, *The English Reformation* (B. T. Batsford Ltd., 1964; Fontana, 1967).

J. Dominian, *Marital Breakdown* (Penguin, 1968).
Christian Marriage (Darton, Longman and Todd, 1967).
Cycles of Affirmation (Darton, Longman and Todd, 1975).
'The Changing Nature of Marriage and Marital Breakdown', *The Clergy Review* (Dec. 1973), p. 926.
The Marriage Relationship Today (Mothers Union, 1974).
'The Christian Response to Marital Breakdown', *Ampleforth Journal, 73/1* (1968), p. 3ff.

H. Dooyeweerd, *A New Critique of Theoretical Thought*, Vol. 3 (Presbyterian and Reformed, ET 1969).

S. R. Driver, *A Critical and Exegetical Commentary on Deuteronomy* (T. & T. Clark, 1895) (ICC reprint, 1951).

G. E. Duffield (ed.), *The Work of Thomas Cranmer* (Sutton Courtenay, 1964).

F. Dulley, *How Christian is Divorce and Remarriage?* (Grove, 1974).

G. R. Dunstan, 'The Marriage Covenant', *Theology* (May 1975), p. 244.
The Artifice of Ethics (SCM, 1974).

G. Duty, *Divorce and Remarriage* (Bethany Fellowship, 1967).

R. J. Ehrlich, 'The Indissolubility of Marriage as a Theological Problem', *Scottish Journal of Theology, 23/3* (1970), p. 291.

L. M. Epstein, *Marriage Laws in the Bible and the Talmud* (Cambridge, 1942).
Sex Laws and Customs in Judaism (1948).

D. Field, *Taking Sides* (IVP, 1975).
T. V. Fleming S.J., 'Christ and Divorce', *Theological Studies*, Vol. 24. No. 1 (1963), p. 106.
R. Fletcher, *The Family and Marriage in Britain* (Penguin, 1962, 1973)[3].
A. Fremantle (ed.), *The Papal Encyclicals* (Mentor, 1956).

M. Geldard, 'Jesus' Teaching on Divorce', *Churchman*, 92/2 (1978), p. 134.
C. Gore, *The Question of Divorce* (J. Murray, 1911).

F. Handley, 'The Pastoral Care of the Married – 2', *The Clergy Review* (May 1976), p. 186.
W. Harrington, 'Jesus' Attitude towards Divorce', *Irish Theological Quarterly*, 37/3 (1970), p. 199.
C. C. Harris, *The Family* (Allen and Unwin, 1969).
G. L. H. Harvey, *The Clergy and Marriage of the Divorced.*
A. Hastings, *Christian Marriage in Africa* (SPCK, 1973).
R. Haw, *The State of Matrimony* (SPCK, 1952).
D. Hill, *The Gospel of Matthew* (Oliphants, 1972).
P. Hocken, 'The Pastoral Care of Mixed Marriages', *The Clergy Review* – I (April 1971), p. 262; II (May 1971), p. 358.
Hooper's Works, Parker Society edition.
J. L. Houlden, *Ethics and the New Testament* (Penguin, 1973).
P. E. Hughes, *Theology of the English Reformers* (Hodder, 1965).

A. Isaksson, *Marriage and Ministry in the New Temple* (Lund, 1965).

P. K. Jewett, *Man as Male and Female* (Eerdmans, 1975).
O. R. Johnston, *Who Needs The Family?* (Hodder, 1979).
Cheslyn Jones (ed.), *For Better, For Worse* (The Church Literature Association, 1977)[2].
M. C. Jones and S. Howarth, *Preparation for Marriage* (Care and Counsel, 1977).
R. Jones, *How Goes Christian Marriage?* (Epworth, 1978).
J. P. Jossua O.P., 'The Fidelity of Love and the Indissolubility of Christian Marriage', *The Clergy Review* (March 1971), p. 172.

G. H. Joyce S.J., *Christian Marriage* (Sheed and Ward, 1948).
E. A. Judge, *The Social Pattern of Christian Groups in the First Century* (Tyndale, 1960).

C. F. Keil and F. Delitzsch, *Biblical Commentary on the Old Testament* The Pentateuch Vol. 3 (Eerdmans, reprint 1971).
K. E. Kirk, *Marriage and Divorce* (Hodder and Stoughton, 1948)[2].
B. Kisembo, L. Magesa, A. Shorter, *African Christian Marriage* (Geoffrey Chapman, 1977).
A. M. Kreykamo P.O., L. Schellevis, L. G. A. von Noort O.S.C., R. Kaptein (tr. I. C. Rottenberg), *Protestant-Catholic Marriage* (The Saint Andrew Press, 1969).
M. & R. Kysar, *The Asundered* (John Knox Press, Atlanta, 1978).

T. A. Lacey, *Marriage in Church and State* (1912), revised edition by R. C. Mortimer (SPCK, 1947).
R. D. Laing, *The Divided Self* (Pelican edition, 1968).
    The Politics of the Family (Pelican, 1976).
G. E. Ladd, *Jesus and the Kingdom* (SPCK, 1966).
W. Lillie, *Studies in New Testament Ethics* (Oliver and Boyd, 1961).
    The Law of Christ (The Saint Andrew Press, 1956; rev. 1966).
J. R. Lucas, 'Frustration and Forgiveness', *Theology* (May 1971).
    'The *Vinculum Conjugale*: a Moral Reality', *Theology* (May 1975), p. 226.
M. Luther, *The Babylonian Captivity of the Church* (1520) in H. T. Lehman (ed.), *Luther's Works* vol. 36 (Fortress Press, 1959).

A. T. MacMillan, *What Is Christian Marriage?* (MacMillan, 1944).
J. Macquarrie, 'The Nature of the Marriage Bond', *Theology* (May 1975), p. 230.
B. Malina, 'Does *Porneia* mean Fornication?', *Novum Testamentum, 14* (1972), p. 10.
J. Marshall, 'Pastoral Care of the Married – 1', *The Clergy Review* (April 1976), p. 149.
P. Martyr, *The Commonplaces* (1583).
W. E. May, 'Marriage and the Church's Task: A Comment', *The Clergy Review* (Sept. 1978), p. 349.
J. Milton, 'The Doctrine and Discipline of Divorce',
    'The Judgement of Martin Bucer concerning Divorce',
    'Tetrachordon',

'Colasterion' in *The Prose Works of John Milton* Vol. 3 (Henry Bohn, London).
J. Murray, *Principles of Conduct* (Tyndale, 1957).
Divorce (Presbyterian and Reformed, 1961).

D. O'Callaghan, 'Theology and Divorce', *Irish Theological Quarterly*, 37 (1970), p. 210.
O. M. T. O'Donovan, 'Marriage and the Family' in B. Kaye (ed.), *Obeying Christ in a Changing World: 3 The Changing World* (Collins Fount, 1977).
Marriage and Permanence (Grove, 1978).
J. H. Olthuis, *I Pledge You My Troth* (Harper and Row, 1976).
'Marriage' in C. F. H. Henry (ed.), *Baker's Dictionary of Christian Ethics* (Baker Book House, 1973).
H. Oppenheimer, *Law and Love* (Faith Press, 1962).
'Is the Marriage Bond an Indissoluble Vinculum?', *Theology* (May 1975), p. 236.
The Marriage Bond (The Faith Press, 1976).
J. Owen, 'Of Marrying after Divorce in case of Adultery' in W. H. Goold (ed.), *The Works of John Owen* vol. 16 (Banner of Truth Trust (reprint), 1968).

Peake's Commentary on the Bible (Nelson, revised edn 1962).
O. A. Piper, *The Biblical View of Sex and Marriage* (Nesbit, 1960).
Pope Pius XI, *Casti Connubii* (1930), published as *Christian Marriage* (Catholic Truth Society, 1964).
V. J. Pospishil, *Divorce and Remarriage: Towards a New Catholic Teaching* (Burns and Oates, 1967).
The First Prayer Book of Edward VI (1549).
The Second Prayer Book of Edward VI (1552).
M. Puxon, *Family Law* (Penguin, 1963, 1971).

Q. Quesnell, 'Made Themselves Eunuchs for the Kingdom of Heaven', *Catholic Biblical Quarterly*, 30 (1968), p. 335.

P. Ramsey, *Basic Christian Ethics* (Scribners, 1950).
Nine Modern Moralists (Prentice Hall, 1962).
Deeds and Rules in Christian Ethics, *Scottish Journal of Theology* Occasional Paper No. 11 (1965).
One Flesh (Grove, 1975).

two unpublished essays:
'Augustine and "the Presiding Mind"', and 'Sex and the Order of Reason in Thomas Aquinas'.

H. Rashdall, *Conscience and Christ* (Duckworth, 1916).

C. O. Rhodes, 'The Liberal Understanding of Marriage and Divorce', *Church Gazette* (Nov.-Dec. 1956), p. 3.

H. Ribberbos, *The Coming of the Kingdom* (Presbyterian and Reformed, 1962, ET 1975).

Rochester, Bishop of (C. Chavasse), *Five Questions Before the Church* (Canterbury Press, 1947).

'Nullity', *The Churchman*, 70/4 (1956), p. 189.

J. P. Sampley, '*And The Two Shall Become One Flesh*' (Cambridge, 1971).

E. Schillebeeckx, *Marriage: Human Reality and Saving Mystery* (Sheed and Ward, 1965).

D. W. Shaner, *A Christian View of Divorce* (Brill, 1969).

A. P. Shepherd, *Marriage Was Made for Man* (Methuen, 1958).

A. C. R. Skynner, *One Flesh: Separate Persons* (Constable, 1976).

L. B. Smedes, *The Reformed Journal* (October 1976), p. 10.

Sex for Christians (Eerdmans, 1977).

B. L. Smith, *Marriage and Divorce in the Light of the Biblical Teaching* (The Australian Lawyers Christian Fellowship).

G. Adam Smith, *The Book of Deuteronomy* (Cambridge, 1918).

D. Stevens, *Marriage: Towards a Christian Understanding and Consensus*, Dolphin papers (CLA, 1976).

R. A. Stewart, *Rabbinic Theology* (Oliver and Boyd, 1961).

J. R. W. Stott, 'The Biblical Teaching on Divorce', *The Churchman*, 85/3 (1971), p. 165.

Christian Counter Culture (IVP, 1978).

S. R. Strong, 'Christian Counselling', *Counselling and Values* (1975).

E. L. H. Taylor, *The Reformational Understanding of Family and Marriage* (Craig Press, 1970).

H. Thielicke, *The Ethics of Sex* (James Clarke, ET, 1964).

B. Thornes and J. Collard, *Who Divorces?* (Routledge and Kegan Paul, 1979).

Tyndale's Doctrinal Treatises, Parker Society edition.

B. Vawter, 'The Divorce Clauses in Matt. 5:32 and 19:9', *Catholic Biblical Quarterly*, 16 (1954), p. 155.

G. von Rad, *Genesis* (SCM, 1961).

Deuteronomy (SCM, 1966).

E. Walsh, 'The Pastoral Care of the Married – 3', *The Clergy Review* (June 1976), p. 237.

M. R. Ward, 'Once Married Always Married?', *The Churchman*, 87/3 (1973), p. 190.

J. Waterworth (tr.), *The Canons and Decrees of the Sacred and Oecumenical Council of Trent* (Dolman, 1848).

O. D. Watkins, *Holy Matrimony* (Rivington, Percival & Co., 1895).

G. J. Wenham, *Marriage and Divorce: The Legal and Social Setting of the Biblical Teaching*. A memorandum submitted to the Church of Ireland Committee on the remarriage of divorced persons. Unpublished, but summarized in *Third Way*, Vol. 1 Nos 20-22 (1977).

Whitgift's Works, Parker Society edition.

M. J. Williams, 'The Man-Woman Relation in the New Testament', *Churchman* (Jan. 1977).

A. R. Winnett, *Divorce and Remarriage in Anglicanism* (Macmillan, 1958).

Divorce and the Church (A. R. Mowbray, 1968).

J. Stafford Wright, 'Marriage and Divorce – Christian Teaching', *Church Gazette* (Nov., Dec. 1956), p. 13.

Zurich Letters, Parker Society edition.

Reports

The Chronicle of Convocation. Record of Proceedings of the Convocation of Canterbury.

Church Assembly *Report of Proceedings.*

General Synod *Report of Proceedings.*

Marriage and Divorce in the Church of England. Memoranda submitted to the Royal Commission (1952).

The Church and the Law of Nullity of Marriage (SPCK, 1955).

Putting Asunder, A Divorce Law for Contemporary Society (SPCK, 1966).

What the Bishops have said about Marriage. Extracts from Lambeth Conference Statements (SPCK, 1968).

Marriage, Divorce and the Church (Chairman: H. Root) (SPCK 1971).

Marriage, Divorce and the Church – A Review, Shaftesbury Project Occasional Paper No. 1 (1971).

A. Hastings, *Christian Marriage in Africa* (SPCK, 1973).

Marriage and the Family in Britain Today. A survey by the General Synod Board for Social Responsibility (CIO, 1974).

Anglican-Roman Catholic Marriage (CIO, 1975).

African Christian Marriage (Geoffrey Chapman, 1977).

The Nottingham Statement (Falcon Books, 1977).

Marriage and the Church's Task (Chairman: The Bishop of Lichfield) (CIO, 1978).

The Theology and Meaning of Marriage (Church Union, 1978).

The Six Lambeth Conferences.

The Church and Marriage – Report of the Joint Committees of the Convocations (1935).

Index